WORLD

UNIT 1	Dallas, Los Angeles, New York, Tokyo
UNIT 2	Beijing, Kawasaki*, Kitakyushu*, Minamata*, Rhode Island*, Tokyo, Yokkaichi*
UNIT 3	Nanmoku, Tokyo
UNIT 4	Tokyo, Washington D.C., Yokohama*
UNIT 5	Antarctica, Florida*, Greenland, Miami, New Jersey*, North Carolina*, Perth (Curtin Univ.), Potsdam, Princeton*, Stanford
UNIT 6	Geneve* (WMO's headquarters), Hiroshima*
UNIT 7	Cupertino* (Apple's headquarters), Mountain View* (Google's headquarters), Redmond* (Microsoft's headquarters), Sunnyvale* (Yahoo!'s headquarters), Tunis (Ibn Khaldun's birthplace)
UNIT 8	Abu Dhabi, Percian (Arabian) gulf
UNIT 9	Bruxelles* (headquarters of the European Commission), London
UNIT10	Buenos Aires, Fukushima*, Istanbul, Lausanne* (I.O.C.'s headquarters), Madrid, Nagano*, Portland*, Sapporo*, Tokyo
UNIT 11	Ankara, Buenos Aires, Istanbul, Lausanne*, Madrid, Montreal (WADA's headquarters), Tokyo
UNIT 12	Massachusetts* (Harvard Univ., M.I.T., Olin College of Engineering), Stanford*
UNIT 13	Geneve*, Glasgow*, New York, Singapore, Venezia (Venice)*
UNIT 14	Arizona*, Baltimore, Illinois*, Mandalay*, Massachusetts*, Naypyidaw*, New York, Washington D.C., Yangon

◇地名に*が付いてるものは裏表紙の見返しの地図を参照

Reading The New York Times 2

ニューヨークタイムズで高める英語と国際教養

Yoshitaka Kozuka
Hideki Watanabe

写真提供

Unit 1 The New York Times / Unit 2 AFP/ Biosphoto / Unit 3 AFP/ EyePress News / Unit 4 The New York Times / Unit 5 AFP/ NASA / Unit 6 AFP/ TORU YAMANAKA / Unit 7 The New York Times, AFP/ TONY AVELAR / Unit 8 AFP/ BERTRAND LANGLOIS / Unit 9 The New York Times, AFP/ BEN STANSALL / Unit 10 AFP/ FABRICE COFFRINI / Unit 11 AFP/ DPA / Unit 12 The New York Times, AFP/ Cultura Creative / Unit 13 AFP/ Biosphoto / Unit 14 AFP/ JEWEL SAMAD

Unit 1	Matsui, Star in Two Continents, Is Retiring (By KEN BELSON, Dec 27, 2012)
Unit 2	Japan's Pollution Diet (By ALEXANDRA HARNEY, Feb 15, 2013)
Unit 3	Without Babies, Can Japan Survive? (By ALEXANDRA HARNEY, Dec 15, 2012)
Unit 4	Safe Food for Japan (By MARTIN FACKLER, Oct 11, 2007)
Unit 5	Timing a Rise in Sea Level (By JUSTIN GILLIS, Aug 12, 2013)
Unit 6	What to Make of a Warming Plateau (By JUSTIN GILLIS, Jun 10, 2013)
Unit 7	The Decline of E-Empires (By PAUL KRUGMAN, Aug 25, 2013)
Unit 8	Abu Dhabi Company Searches for Greener Method of Desalination (By SARA HAMDAN, Jan 23, 2013)
Unit 9	British Employers See Value in Europe-Wide Labor Pool (By STEPHEN CASTLE, Jun 7, 2013)
Unit 10	Hopes for Renewal in Japan, but Also a Host of Challenges (By HIROKO TABUCHI and JOSHUA HUNT, Sept 7, 2013)
Unit 11	Madrid and Istanbul Respond Differently to Rejection by Olympics (By RAPHAEL MINDER and CEYLAN YEGINSU, Sept 8, 2013)
Unit 12	Need a Job? Invent It (By THOMAS L. FRIEDMAN, Mar 30, 2013)
Unit 13	Arts Education in Singapore Moves to Center Stage (By KRISTIANO ANG, May 26, 2013)
Unit 14	Myanmar's Educators Reach Out to the World (By LARA FARRAR, May 5, 2013)

Reading The New York Times 2

Copyright © 2014 by Yoshitaka Kozuka, Hideki Watanabe

*All rights reserved for Japan.
No part of this book may be reproduced in any form
without permission from Seibido Co., Ltd.*

Permission for use of the articles and logo has been granted by The New York Times Syndicate. All opinions expressed by the authors and publisher are their own and do not necessarily reflect the opinions of the journalists, editors, publishers or editorial boards of The New York Times.

はしがき

　本書は、最近のThe New York Timesの記事を題材とした時事英語教材の続編である。前作と同じく、コミュニケーション力を高めるには精読が基礎となるという信念の下、リーディングを中心に据えつつ他の三技能の要素も盛り込み全体を構成した。

　収録した記事は「日本に学ぶ世界」、「環境」、「経済」、「オリンピック」、「教育」の5つのテーマに関する14本である。記事の舞台はアジア、アメリカ、ヨーロッパを始め実に幅広い。扱う話題はどれも一過性ではなく、普遍的で継続的、そして多面的である。また、現代を理解し、これからの世界を考える上で非常に重要な内容となっている。

　新聞というと無味乾燥な事実報告という印象を持つかもしれないが、収録したどの記事にも著者の生きたメッセージが込められている。皆さんにはそれを丹念に能動的に読み解いて欲しいし、そうでなければ読むことにはならない。このような思いから、考える手間や辞書を引く手間を省くだけの語註は付けなかった。わからないことばに出会ったら、まずは立ち止まって辞書を引き、考えよう。

　記事を深く読み込むことは、狭義の英語力だけでなく、現代においてはそれと不可分の二つの素養の向上にもつながるだろう。第一にメディアリテラシーである。メディアが伝えるのは純粋なる事実ではなく、作り手による事実の切り取りや解釈である。日本のメディアを通じて把握していることが、海外のメディアではどう捉えられ伝えられているか、その違いを通してメディアの特性を実感しよう。

　第二に異文化理解である。グローバル化社会と言われる現在、インターネットや交通の発達により、自分とは異なる環境にある他者との交流がかつてないほど身近になった。そうした時代においては、積極的に発信する態度とともに、他者を理解し尊重しようとする姿勢が一層重要性を増す。様々な地域や立場の事情に目を向け、じっくり考えることで他者への眼差しが養われると期待する。

　このような理念と目標に基づく学習を実現するために、本書では皆さんの学習を支援する様々な手立てを準備した。詳細は「本書の構成」に述べたので、随時参照して本書を有効に利用してもらいたい。

　本書の作成に当たり、成美堂社長佐野英一郎氏、営業部田村栄一氏を始め同社スタッフの皆様には、趣旨をご理解頂き、多大なるご支援を頂いた。末筆ながら厚く御礼申し上げる次第である。

2014年晩夏　　編者しるす

本書の構成

本書は、学習の一助として以下のような手立てを提供している。

◇ **Keywords**
ユニット冒頭に、内容に関わる最重要語句（A）と難易度の高い語句（B）をそれぞれ10ずつ挙げた。本文中ではAは太字にし、Bには下線が引いてある。骨のある英文であるが、この20の語句をしっかり押さえておけばスムーズに入っていけるだろう。

◇ **Exercises**
・Exercise 1
登場する人物や事項に関する英語でのＱ＆Ａ。本文中の表現を使って説明してみよう。読んでインプットした表現を「使う情報」として捉え直し、口にすることで、アウトプットの練習になるとともに、表現の理解を深めることにもつながるだろう。

・Exercise 2
内容レビューの問題。記事のポイントを振り返ることができるような問いを3つ立てた。問いを頭に置いて読み返すことで、内容の理解度を高めよう。

・Exercise 3, 4
音声を使ったエクササイズ。本文中の表現をできる限りそのまま使って作られた要約文を聴いて空所補充やシャドーイングを行う。読解で繰り返し目にした表現に音として改めて触れることで、リスニング力だけでなく語彙力を始めとする表現力も高まるだろう。

◇ 理解を深めるための参考資料
・コラム
ユニットの最後に、内容と関連する補足情報やエピソードなどを紹介した。随時読んで記事の理解を深めよう。

・地図
見返しに2種類掲載した。表紙側が世界地図、裏表紙側が一部地域の拡大図である。本文に登場する国や都市、また、主だった施設や機関の所在地を示した。地理情報から見えてくることも多いので、随時参照しよう。

・Keywords List
巻末に2種類掲載した。一つは、各ユニットのキーワードの一覧（List I）で、もう一つは、複数のユニットに出現するキーワードの一覧（List II）である。List IIには出現ユニットを全て示してある。復習などに活用しよう。

Contents

Chapter 1 日本に学ぶ世界
- **Unit 1** Matsui, Star in Two Continents, Is Retiring
  松井秀喜選手引退 1
- **Unit 2** Japan's Pollution Diet
  中国の環境汚染・日本の取組み 7
- **Unit 3** Without Babies, Can Japan Survive?
  日本の少子化を憂う 13
- **Unit 4** Safe Food for Japan
  アメリカが注目する日本の食品安全基準 19

Chapter 2 環境
- **Unit 5** Timing a Rise in Sea Level
  極地の氷が解ければ海面上昇 25
- **Unit 6** What to Make of a Warming Plateau
  最近10年は温暖化の停滞期? 31

Chapter 3 経済
- **Unit 7** The Decline of E-Empires
  IT帝国の落日 37
- **Unit 8** Abu Dhabi Company Searches for Greener Method of Desalination
  水がただになる日 43
- **Unit 9** British Employers See Value in Europe-Wide Labor Pool
  グローバル化の功罪 49

Chapter 4 オリンピック
- **Unit 10** Hopes for Renewal in Japan, but Also a Host of Challenges
  オリンピックは来たけれど 55
- **Unit 11** Madrid and Istanbul Respond Differently to Rejection by Olympics
  オリンピックを招致するということ 61

Chapter 5 教育
- **Unit 12** Need a Job? Invent It
  「仕事を創る」という発想 67
- **Unit 13** Arts Education in Singapore Moves to Center Stage
  生きる力につながる芸術教育 73
- **Unit 14** Myanmar's Educators Reach Out to the World
  世界が関心を寄せるミャンマーの教育改革 79

Keywords List 85

UNIT 1: Matsui, Star in Two Continents, Is Retiring

松井秀喜選手引退

By KEN BELSON December 27, 2012

スポーツの世界でも国際化が進み、野茂英雄投手以来アメリカへ渡って活躍する選手が増えている。読売ジャイアンツの4番打者だった松井選手はメジャーリーグ、ヤンキースでもスターとなった。アメリカ人は松井選手のどこに惹かれるのか。

KEYWORDS

CD 1 - 02, 03

A. 記事読解に特に重要な語句の意味を確認しよう。

1. manage
2. scrutiny
3. billing
4. swan song
5. sideline
6. cleanup
7. understatement
8. homage
9. acclimate
10. blend in

B. 上下の語群で意味の近いものを結び付け、記事に現れる難易度の高い語句の言い換えを確認しよう。

1. hallowed ( )
2. equivalent ( )
3. anointed ( )
4. nod ( )
5. fuss ( )
6. bang ( )
7. welling up ( )
8. committed ( )
9. groomed ( )
10. irk ( )

a. excitement	b. honored	c. big success	d. similar
e. full of tears	f. selected	g. dedicated	h. prepared
i. irritate	j. acknowledgement		

1

1 Like the United States, Japan has its own baseball royalty, and the princes are high school players drafted by the Yomiuri Giants. Being chosen by the hallowed Giants—Japan's equivalent of the Yankees, the Lakers and the Cowboys combined does not guarantee success. But the princes who succeed on and off the field are all but certain to be anointed kings.

2 Some of Japan's most beloved players include Shigeo Nagashima, Sadaharu Oh and Tatsunori Hara, who all starred for the Giants and later **managed** the team. Hara just guided the Giants to their 22nd championship, easily the most in Japanese baseball.

3 Hideki Matsui was destined to follow them. After a stellar high school career, Matsui was chosen by the Giants and made his debut in 1993 to much fanfare. His powerful bat earned him the nickname Godzilla, and he wore No. 55, a nod to Oh's single-season home run record. Under intense **scrutiny**, he lived up to the **billing**, hitting 332 homers in 10 seasons. He led the Giants to three titles, including in 2002, when he won the Most Valuable Player award.

4 It was his **swan song** in Japan. Matsui, the humble country boy who gave his all, who never raised a fuss and made grandmothers across the country proud, became a free agent and joined the Yankees the next year. Japan was torn. He was at the height of his powers, yet he headed to New York to play on baseball's biggest stage. "I tried to tell myself I needed to stay here for the prosperity of Japanese baseball," he said in a nationally televised news conference a decade ago. But "I will do my best there so the fans will be glad I went."

5 No doubt, Japanese fans were glad he went. Matsui hit a grand slam in his first game at Yankee Stadium, in 2003, and he helped the Yankees return to the World Series that year. He played in every game his first three seasons before injuries **sidelined** him. He finished with a bang, hitting three homers in the 2009 World Series, which the Yankees won; he was named the most valuable player.

6 Matsui played with the Angels, the Athletics and the Rays in the last three seasons, but he was a far smaller presence. On Thursday, he conceded to the inevitable when he announced his retirement in a room packed with Japanese reporters at a Midtown Manhattan hotel. "I wanted to bat **cleanup** again, but the results weren't there," Matsui said in slow, quiet Japanese, his eyes seemingly welling up. "I thought it was time to stop."

7 With characteristic **understatement**, Matsui said he had no regrets, only that he could not play better. He paid **homage** to Nagashima, his manager on the Giants, who told him that Joe DiMaggio had also played center field, where Matsui played in Tokyo. Ever polite, he refused to name a favorite teammate so as not to leave anyone out.

8 Derek Jeter was not as shy. "I've had a lot of teammates over the years with the Yankees, but I will always consider Hideki one of my favorites," Jeter said in a statement. "Despite being shadowed by a large group of reporters, having the pressures of performing for his fans both in New York and Japan and becoming **acclimated** to the bright lights of New York City, he always remained focused and committed to his job and to those of us he shared the clubhouse with."

9 Matsui declined to say what he planned to do next. But given his even temper and reputation, managing in Japan is a natural choice. "I guess managing, he has the ability to do that," said George Rose, who translated for Matsui when he came to America and is an adviser to the Yankees. "Younger players would really relate well to him."

10 If Matsui had stayed with the Giants, he would have been groomed to take over as manager. But his departure for America irked the Giants, who tried hard to keep him. Though Hideo Nomo, Ichiro Suzuki and many other Japanese moved to America before him, Matsui was the first star from the Giants to leave. His decision not to play for Japan in the World Baseball Classic also made waves.

11 The question may be irrelevant because Matsui appears comfortable living in the United States, said Robert Whiting, who has written extensively about Japanese baseball. Here, he can **blend in** and raise a family without being chased by ever-present reporters. "Still, I somehow think that all would be forgiven if Matsui wanted to come back to Japan," Whiting said. "Matsui has a lot of capital to spend in Japan." (775 words)

NOTES

タイトル Star in Two Continents　日本は島国であるので、「日米のプロ野球でスターであった」の意味での Two Continents は実は不正確である。Asian & American というような意味であろう。

ll.3-4 the Lakers and the Cowboys　Dallas Cowboys はプロアメリカンフットボール、Los Angeles Lakers はプロバスケットボール、New York Yankees はメジャーリーグプロ野球の名門でファンが多い。

ll.6-7 Shigeo Nagashima, Sadaharu Oh　長嶋茂雄は王貞治と共に川上哲治が監督をしていた巨人軍で中軸打者を務めて巨人日本シリーズ9連覇に貢献した。2013年5月5日に松井秀喜と共に国民栄誉賞を受賞した。

l.7 starred　動詞が r で終わり、その最終音節にストレスがある時は、過去形や 〜ing 形で r を重ねることに注意。barred, referred, stirred, abhorred, occurred（Unit 3, l.28）など。

l.8 easily the most　2012年のクライマックスシリーズ、ファイナルステージでは2位の中日と対戦し3連敗で王手をかけられた後に巨人が3連勝で、日本シリーズ進出を決めた。日本ハムとの日本シリーズは4勝2敗で3年ぶり22度目の日本一を達成した。

l.10 stellar　形容詞 stellar の原義は「星の、星に関する」で、名詞 star に「人気者、スター」の意味があるように「スターの、花形の」の意味を持つ。「小さい星」の意の starlet に「売り出し中若手スター」、supernova「超新星」に「超人気者、スーパースター」の比喩義があることも参照。

l.11 to much fanfare　"to the fanfare" は「ファンファーレに合わせて」の意で、"despite the fanfare"「ファンファーレにもかかわらず」のように民衆の喝采について言う表現。ここは "with much fanfare" とほぼ同義。

l.13 home run record　2013年7月28日にヤンキースタジアムで行われた松井選手引退セレモニーでは、主将のジーターから松井に背番号55のユニホームが贈られた。

l.16 humble　松井選手が慎み深いのは有名で、本記事の後半にも出てくるが、ホームランを打ってガッツポーズをすることもなく、自分の記録の自慢もしない。2013年の国民栄誉賞受賞の報を受けて米国人ファンや元同僚が humble という言葉を口にするのを、米メディアは何度も流した。

l.17 made grandmothers across the country proud　"This beats my grandmother."（口語）「こいつは驚いた」、"shoot one's grandmother"（口語）「がっかりさせる」などと比較して、「このような立派な野球選手がいると、日本中の人々が自慢に思った」のような意味であろう。

l.18 torn　「分裂する、意見が割れる」の意では他に動詞 divide, split, splinter などが良く使われる。世論がほぼ五分五分に割れて政治的な決着がつかない状態を "split down the middle" ばらばらに分かれているのを "badly splintered" などと表す。

l.23 grand slam　"grand slam" は本来、スポーツで年間の主要な試合全部に優勝することを意味し、テニスでは全英・全仏・全豪・全米に優勝することであるが、野球では満塁ホームランのこと。

l.37 Joe DiMaggio　ジョー・ディマジオはベーブ・ルース引退後の1936年にヤンキースと契約し、ルー・ゲーリッグが途中で引退した1939年には初のMVPと首位打者を獲得して、ヤンキースのナンバーワンプレーヤーになった。グラウンドでの態度やファンへの誠実な対応は、野球選手の鑑とされた。ディマジオの兄弟二人もメジャーリーグ選手で全員センター（中堅手）であったのは有名。

Unit 1 Matsui, Star in Two Continents, Is Retiring

EXERCISES

1 本文に基づいて以下の問いに英語で答えなさい。

1. What does 55, Matsui's uniform number, acknowledge?

2. How many homers did Matsui hit in the 2009 World Series?

3. Who told Matsui that Joe DiMaggio had also played center field?

2 本文に基づいて以下の問いに答えなさい。

1. アメリカへ渡る前の松井選手の成績はどのようなものでしたか。

2. 松井選手の品行方正や慎み深さを表す表現を抜き出しなさい。

3. この記事では、様々な人のインタビューを通じて、松井選手の評価をしています。これについてまとめてみましょう。

3 CDを聴いて以下の要約文の空欄に適語を入れなさい。

Hideki Matsui, nicknamed Godzilla for his powerful batting, made his debut for the Giants in 1993. He hit 332 (　　　　　) in 10 seasons, and led the Giants to three titles. In 2003 he joined the New York Yankees. In his first game at Yankee Stadium, he hit a grand slam. In the 2009 World Series, which the Yankees won, he hit three homers and was named most (　　　　　) player. After leaving the Yankees, he played three more seasons with other teams before (　　　　　). Yankees' star Derek Jeter considered Matsui one of his favorite teammates. If Matsui had stayed with the Giants, he may have become their (　　　　　). Sports writer Robert Whiting thinks Matsui may enjoy being comfortable living in the States because he can (　　　　　) in and raise a family without being bothered by reporters.

4 CDをもう一度聴いてシャドーイングしてみよう。

COLUMN

　アメリカの野球の試合中に観客によって歌われる *Take Me Out to The Ball Game*「私を野球に連れてって」で分かるとおり、ふつうは野球の試合を ball game、球場を ball park と略式に表すが、球場を意味する名詞は National League と American League の29チームのホームグラウンドで field, park, stadium が9個ずつ、他は dome と coliseum が一つずつである。イチロー選手が初め所属していたシアトル・マリナーズのホームは Safeco Field、松坂投手が在籍したボストン・レッドソックスのホームは Fenway Park、松井選手が活躍したニューヨーク・ヤンキースは Yankee Stadium である。
　明治以来の日本人の野球の受容や日米野球の相違について知りたいならば、簡単に入手できる本（新書）として以下のものがある。玉木正之、ロバート・ホワイティング著『ベースボールと野球道』（講談社現代新書）、伊東一雄・馬立勝著『野球は言葉のスポーツ』（中公新書）、平出隆著『白球礼讃』（岩波新書）、池井優著『野球と日本人』（丸善ライブラリー）。

UNIT 2

Japan's Pollution Diet

中国の環境汚染・日本の取組み

By ALEXANDRA HARNEY   February 15, 2013

高度成長期の日本では環境への配慮が後回しとなり、川は汚れて魚が住まなくなり、晴れた日には光化学スモッグが発生した。現在中国では急激な経済発展の中、環境汚染が深刻化している。きれいな水と土壌、空気を取り戻す道はあるのか。

KEYWORDS

CD 1 - 10, 11

A. 記事読解に特に重要な語句の意味を確認しよう。

1. habitation
2. carbon monoxide
3. asthma
4. mercury poisoning
5. proactive
6. electoral system
7. pander
8. U.S.-Japan Security Treaty
9. acknowledge
10. carcinogen

B. 上下の語群で意味の近いものを結び付け、記事に現れる難易度の高い語句の言い換えを確認しよう。

1. wreathed   (　)   2. lift   (　)   3. annual   (　)
4. excruciating (　)   5. spotless   (　)   6. leeway   (　)
7. blizzard   (　)   8. obstacle   (　)   9. toxic   (　)
10. incineration (　)

a. burning	b. covered	c. problem	d. series or succession
e. yearly	f. poisonous	g. fine and clean	h. move
i. freedom	j. painful		

1 TOKYO—Seeing Beijing <u>wreathed</u> in smog throughout the winter, it has been hard not to worry about the costs of China's rapid economic growth. As Jon Stewart pointed on The Daily Show: Can't a country capable of <u>lifting</u> hundreds of millions of people out of poverty find a way to keep its own capital safe for **habitation**?

2 Five decades ago, people were asking similar questions about Japan. Even as the world marveled at the country's 10 percent <u>annual</u> growth, alarm was growing over air pollution in several cities. Emissions of nitrogen dioxide, **carbon monoxide** and sulfur dioxide tripled during the 1960s. Japan became known for pollution-related illnesses: Yokkaichi **asthma**, Minamata disease (**mercury poisoning**) — both named after the cities where they first appeared—and cadmium poisoning, known as itai-itai, or "ouch-ouch," because of the <u>excruciating</u> bone pain it caused.

3 Today, Japanese cities are among the world's least polluted, according to the World Health Organization. Japan's environmental record is hardly <u>spotless</u>, but the country rightly prides itself on blue skies, Prius taxis and mandatory recycling. What's more, it managed to clean up without sacrificing growth by investing in pollution-control technologies and giving local governments <u>leeway</u> to tighten standards beyond national requirements.

4 It wasn't easy. The Liberal Democratic Party, which governed Japan almost continuously from 1955 to 2009 and returned to power in December, wasn't **proactive** in cleaning up the country's air and water. That's partly because until the mid-1990s Japan's **electoral system** incited politicians to **pander** to the interests of business. With candidates from the same party required to also run against one another, most politicians stood little chance of distinguishing themselves on policy and so tried to secure votes by courting business and industry associations.

5 It was only when citizens' movements, which grew out of protests against the 1960 **U.S.-Japan Security Treaty** and the Vietnam War, got the attention of opposition parties in the 1960s and early 1970s that the government was forced to confront pollution. "I saw the government and L.D.P. as responding just enough, just in time, when the pressure got strong enough that they could defuse the opposition and stay in power," said Timothy George, a professor at the University of Rhode Island and the author of a book on Minamata disease.

6 The first result was a <u>blizzard</u> of laws—14 passed at once—in what became known as the Pollution Diet of 1970. Air pollution fell dramatically in the years that followed. But <u>obstacles</u> remained. It wasn't until 1968, a dozen years after Minamata disease was discovered, that the government **acknowledged** that it was caused by <u>toxic</u> waste dumping by the chemical company Chisso. As late as the 1990s, Japan did not fully comply with some of its own standards. Regulations on the emissions of dioxin, a **carcinogen** produced during <u>incineration</u>, were also pitifully inadequate, particularly for a country that burns most of its trash. And the courts, under political pressure to protect business interests, have taken too long to process pollution cases.

7 Another enduring problem has been Japan's focus on infrastructure development, which causes ecological destruction, to build support from voters. Even today as the population shrinks, politicians spend enthusiastically on building dams, paving hillsides and fortifying shorelines—what Alex Kerr, the author of the book "Dogs and Demons," calls "Japan's rampant and escalating assault on its rivers, mountains and coasts."

8 And yet Japan is a much healthier place to live today than in the 1960s. It cleaned up in part by convincing academia and business that potential profits lay in resolving environmental problems. Kitakyushu—a city in northern Kyushu where chemical and heavy industries contaminated a local bay so badly it became known as the "Sea of Death"— is now a pioneer in the use of hydrogen as a power source. Kawasaki has rebranded itself as an eco-city, building Japan's largest solar power plant on landfill and turning recycling waste into a business. Chisso, once known for dumping toxic waste in the sea, has developed innovative wastewater-treatment technology.

9 The problems caused by pollution are hitting China even harder and faster. But at least in theory it has a late-mover's advantage. Already, thousands of citizens' groups around China have organized to protest against polluting projects, like chemical and copper plants and wastewater pipelines, sometimes even filing lawsuits. The Chinese media are covering these issues more aggressively than in the past.

10 And the government is responding. Last month, it ordered the temporary closure of more than 100 polluting factories and the removal of 30 percent of government vehicles from the streets of Beijing. With the health of a nation of more than one billion people at stake, however, it will have to do much, much more. (801 words)

> **NOTES**
>
> **l.25 stood little chance**　可能性のあることは"stand a fair/good chance of ～ing"、ないことを"stand a ghost of/no chance" でよく表す。
>
> **l.33 defuse**　動詞 defuse は「爆弾の信管を取り除く」という原義を持ち、「緊張・対立を緩和する」という比喩義で国際関係や政治的対立の描写に頻用される（例：The early release of the crew alone would defuse this crisis, as things now stand.「（捕虜になった）乗組員たちが早い段階で解放されたので、現状から見て、今回の危機は回避されるであろう」）。
>
> **l.36 Pollution Diet of 1970**　昭和45年7月に内閣総理大臣を長とする公害対策本部と関係閣僚からなる公害対策閣僚会議が設けられて、公害問題の検討に入り、11月24日からの臨時国会は公害関係14法案が提出され可決された。翌年、現在の環境省である環境庁が設置されることとなる。
>
> **l.38 Minamata disease**　2013年4月には最高裁判決で、行政の審査を覆して患者認定がなされたが（1977年に死亡した溝口チエさん）、環境省は謝罪や認定基準の見直しは行わない方針である。
>
> **l.39 as late as**　類似頻出表現に "as early as ～"「～には既に、～という早い時期に」がある（例："Airplane" is preferred to "aeroplane" in American usage, having received official sanction in Army publications as early as 1918.「米語では飛行機を意味する airplane は aeroplane よりも好まれており、早くも1918年には軍関係の文書でこちらが使われるようになった」）。
>
> **l.48 Alex Kerr**　Alex Kerr 氏は長く日本に滞在して美術や伝統芸能に親しみ、四国の祖谷渓や丹波の亀岡などに住み、京都の町屋の保存運動にも関わっている。簡単に読める本には『美しき日本の残像』（朝日新聞出版）がある。
>
> **l.66 the government is responding**　中国政府は大気中の粒子状物質PM2.5汚染被害に対応して、第12次5カ年計画期間中（2011〜2015）に、火力発電所から出る窒素酸化物を1立方メートル当たり200ミリグラム以下に抑える方針を打ち出した。中国では河川の汚染も深刻な問題であり、レアアース精製工場から沁み出た有害廃棄物が黄河を汚染し、化学工場や製紙工場からの排水垂れ流しで汚染が深刻化した淮河（わいが）流域では癌患者が多く出ている。

Unit 2 Japan's Pollution Diet

EXERCISES

1 本文に基づいて以下の問いに英語で答えなさい。

1. What is the cause of Minamata Disease?

2. When was the air pollution in Japan dramatically controlled and decreased?

3. How has the city of Kitakyushu been changed?

2 本文に基づいて以下の問いに答えなさい。

1. 長く政権にあった自民党が、国の環境改善策を積極的に採ってこなかった理由として挙げられていることを説明しなさい。

2. 高度成長期の日本で、公害に苦しんだ地域として挙げられているのはどこですか。

3. 日本の環境問題として公害以外に挙げられていることは何ですか。

3　CDを聴いて以下の要約文の空欄に適語を入れなさい。

Beijing has such a bad smog problem that some worry whether it is safe for human (　　　　　). Japan had the same problem five decades ago, with many people suffering from pollution-related illnesses. But Japanese cities are now some of the least (　　　　　), and Japan managed to clean up without sacrificing growth. Pressure on the government from citizens' groups helped pass anti-pollution laws, and companies (　　　　　) that they could profit from solving environmental problems. Previously polluted cities such as Kitakyushu and Kawasaki have become (　　　　　) friendly. Problems caused by pollution are now hitting China severely. Citizens' groups and the media, however, are putting pressure on the government to take action. Last month, it (　　　　　) closed more than 100 polluting factories and removed 30 percent of government vehicles from Beijing's streets.

4　CDをもう一度聴いてシャドーイングしてみよう。

COLUMN

　2013年末には中国広東省の夕刊紙「羊城晩報」の記者が中国青年メディア関係者代表団の訪日活動に参加して、日本滞在中に、政府や市民など日本社会が中国の大気汚染問題に極めて高い関心を寄せていることを実感したと同紙が伝えている。この訪日活動では東京大学先端科学技術センターの竹川暢之准教授の講座が特別に設けられて、日本の大気汚染と対策面での利害に関する説明を聞いた。
　20世紀の世界環境事件として、ベルギー・ミューズ渓谷の亜硫酸ガス大気汚染、米国ロサンジェルス光化学スモッグ、米国ペンシルヴァニア州ドノラ大気汚染、英国ロンドンのスモッグ、日本水俣病、日本四日市喘息、日本カネミ油症、日本富山のイタイイタイ病が8大公害とされている。
　日本カネミ油症事件とは、北九州市小倉区のカネミ倉庫で作られた食用油カネミライスオイルの製造過程で、脱臭のために使用されていたポリ塩化ビフェニルが配管作業ミスで漏れて混入し、これが加熱されて変化したダイオキシンによる。油を通してダイオキシンを摂取した人々に、顔面の色素沈着、肌の異常、頭痛、手足のしびれ、肝機能障害などが起きた。妊娠中に油を摂取した患者からは、色素沈着の赤ん坊が生まれ、母乳によって新生児の皮膚が黒くなったケースもあった。「黒い赤ちゃん」は事件の象徴である。

UNIT 3 — Without Babies, Can Japan Survive?

日本の少子化を憂う

By ALEXANDRA HARNEY

December 15, 2012

1990年の1.57ショック以来、日本の出生率は低迷している。2005年には過去最低の1.26となり、2012年には16年ぶりに1.41まで回復したが、非婚化晩婚化も進んで厳しい状況にある。政府はどのような政策をたてているのか、子供の数を増やす道はあるのか。

KEYWORDS

CD 1 - 18, 19

A. 記事読解に特に重要な語句の意味を確認しよう。

1. plight
2. depopulating
3. parliamentary election
4. beneficiaries
5. baby diapers
6. hinterland
7. largess
8. malaise
9. affordable
10. conservative politicians

B. 上下の語群で意味の近いものを結び付け、記事に現れる難易度の高い語句の言い換えを確認しよう。

1. abandon ( )   2. reside ( )   3. stagnation ( )
4. challenges ( )   5. lavish ( )   6. prolonged ( )
7. subsidize ( )   8. dismantle ( )   9. incentives ( )
10. shrink ( )

a. decrease	b. encouragement	c. waste	d. continuing
e. give money to	f. give up	g. live in	h. depression
i. problems	j. knock down		

[1] THE first grade class at the elementary school in Nanmoku, about 85 miles from Tokyo, has just a single student this year. The local school system that five decades ago taught 1,250 elementary school children is now educating just 37. Many of the town's elegant wooden homes are <u>abandoned</u>. Where generations of cedar loggers, sweet potato farmers and factory workers once made their lives, monkeys now <u>reside</u>. The only sounds at night are the cries of deer and the wail of an occasional ambulance.

[2] Nanmoku's **plight** is Japan's fate. Faced with an aging society, a **depopulating** countryside and economic <u>stagnation</u>, the country has struggled for decades to address its <u>challenges</u>. As Japan goes to the polls on Dec. 16 for **parliamentary elections** that will most likely mean the seventh prime minister in six years, voters need to demand that politicians address the most important issue of all: the country's low birthrate.

[3] Sadly, this issue is hardly being discussed on the campaign trail. Instead, parties are promising to <u>lavish</u> more money on special interests like construction companies, the main **beneficiaries** of public works spending. Nowhere is the rapid aging of Japan more visible than in rural towns like Nanmoku, where 56 percent of local residents are over 65. Over the next 25 years, the proportion of Japan's population that is elderly will rise from almost one in four to one in three. Sales of adult diapers will soon surpass those of **baby diapers**.

[4] The reason for Japan's plight stretches back decades. The countryside lost people to the cities during Japan's era of rapid growth between the early 1950s and the late 1980s. The population in rural areas continued to decline even after the country's growth began to slow in the early 1990s. To secure the rural vote, the Liberal Democratic Party, which held power almost continuously from 1955 until 2009, devoted huge amounts of the state's budget to infrastructure projects that were intended to revitalize the **hinterland**. But the revitalization never occurred. Towns were left with deserted train stations, empty hot-spring resorts and extraordinary levels of debt.

[5] Just as America has its military-industrial complex, Japan—whose constitution forbids a formal army—has its "construction state." Public **largess** went to pouring concrete across the country. It's clear now that Japan should have been less focused on building bridges to nowhere and more focused on making babies.

6 Although Japanese couples consistently say in surveys that they would like to have more than two children, they don't. Part of the problem is Japan's prolonged economic **malaise**. Years of stagnant (or declining) incomes have made Japanese men less attractive as potential partners. And economic uncertainty has led couples to delay getting married and having children. The shortage of public day care centers, especially in cities, has made the cost and burden of parenthood so high that today's couples either have fewer babies or none at all. (Japan's birthrate is just 1.39 children per woman.)

7 The government provides subsidized day care, but there is a long waiting list in big cities. Working parents often end up paying more to send their kids to private centers. While there is no exact international comparison, a 2009 survey by the Japanese government found that the first five years of child rearing, including savings, cost around $73,000, more than 2.5 times as much as in the United States.

8 Japan could address its baby shortage by taking three basic steps that have been discussed for years but have never enjoyed sufficient political leadership to be enacted. First, the government must create more subsidized public day care centers, which would make child care more **affordable** for more people.

9 Second, companies must dismantle old systems that promote employees on seniority, rather than skills. These antiquated practices hold down young workers' salaries and keep the labor market too rigid. And companies should discourage overtime work so that employees have more time with their families.

10 Third, both the government and companies should encourage more women to enter the labor force with high-quality jobs on a par with men and offer incentives to women to return to work after childbirth. In places where these sorts of reforms have taken hold, from France to Sweden, the result has been a boost to the birthrate and the economy.

11 To be sure, an increase in the birthrate is no quick fix. Even if Japan were to increase its birthrate next year, it would take at least a generation before the country began to tackle its demographic imbalances. The only shortcut would be a significant increase in immigration, a deeply controversial subject in Japan. **Conservative politicians** and right-wing groups are opposed to bringing in more workers from overseas, and some Japanese worry that foreigners would not assimilate well.

12 The lesson of Nanmoku is that spending one's way out of a crisis doesn't work without reforms that address the root causes of the malaise. Until Japan's leaders take steps to boost the birthrate, the whole country—like the countryside—will continue to shrink. (831 words)

NOTES

l.1 Nanmoku　「南牧村（なんもくむら）」群馬県南西部の人口約2,700人の村、平成17年の国勢調査で三重県紀和町と並んで高齢化日本一となった。妙義荒船佐久高原国定公園に一部が属する急峻な山々に囲まれ、三段の滝・線ヶ滝・象ヶ滝の三滝、黒瀧山不動寺、美しい季節の花々などで有名。長野県の南牧村（みなみまきむら）とは別。

l.8 aging society　「高齢化社会」名詞 age は世の中については時代、人については年齢を表し、特に、成人と高齢に焦点が当たっているので、come of age「成人になる」、the aged「高齢者」、underage「未成年」のような表現が頻用される。動詞 age は「年を取る、熟成する」の意味で用いられる。なお「老齢の、高齢の」の意では日本語のシルバーに対して、英語では gray が用いられることに注意（gray society, gray households）。

l.28 deserted train stations　鉄道の廃線の原因のひとつとして沿線人口の減少がある。1960～70年代は鉱業、林業の衰退と離農の増加など産業構造の変化が主であったが、21世紀の今日では少子化によって、車の運転ができず毎日乗るという地域の主な鉄道利用者の高校生が減少したことが大きいという。

l.30 military-industrial complex　アメリカの Dwight Eisenhower 大統領が1961年1月の離任演説で用いた言葉。軍部、軍需産業、議会との複合的体制を指す（略号MIC）。Eisenhower はそれが国家社会に及ぼす影響力についての懸念と、その力を調整すべきことを述べた。

l.33 nowhere　ここでは「何もないところ、田舎」の意。

ll.41-42 Japan's birthrate　日本の出生率（fertility rate とも）の低さについて国民の間に問題意識が起きたのは前年1989年の数値が1.57であることがわかった1990年で、「1.57ショック」と呼ばれた。以来20年以上低迷を続けている。

ll.53-54 companies must dismantle old systems that promote employees on seniority, rather than skills　高度成長期からの日本の大企業の lifetime employment「終身（生涯）雇用制度」は seniority system「年功序列」に基づいて日本社会の発展を促進したが、バブル崩壊後には続々と meritocracy, performance-based pay「能力主義」に転じている。

l.54 antiquated　「時代遅れの」の意味の類語にはどのようなものがあるだろうか。

l.70 the malaise　国や社会の発展、衰退は人の心身の好調、不調にたとえられる。例えば、日本の開国後の急速な欧化を feverish drive（熱にうかされたような猛進）としたり、高齢化の社会で葬儀業が景気の良い様子を alive and kicking（元気でぴんぴんしている）と死の反義語で表したり、長く続く少子化現象を chronic ailment（日本の慢性疾患）と治療が必要であると述べるなど。

Unit 3 Without Babies, Can Japan Survive?

EXERCISES

1 本文に基づいて以下の問いに英語で答えなさい。

1. What are left in rural towns which the government intended to revitalize?
   _____
   _____

2. In order to boost its birthrate what should the government provide?
   _____
   _____

3. What is Japan suffering due to its declining birthrate?
   _____
   _____

2 本文に基づいて以下の問いに答えなさい。

1. もっと子供が生まれるようになるため、政府がすべき早急の対策として何が挙げられていますか。
   _____
   _____
   _____

2. 少子化と高齢化が同時に進んでいることを示す例として挙げられた品物は何ですか。
   _____
   _____
   _____

3. 本記事では日本の出生率の低下を報じ、増やすための対策を述べていますので、「減る・不足」と「増やす・助長」という意味の語句が、何度か言い換えられて出てきます。それらの類語を抜き出して比較しましょう。
   _____
   _____
   _____

3 CDを聴いて以下の要約文の空欄に適語を入れなさい。

Japan's society is rapidly aging. Over the next 25 years, the proportion of Japan's population that is (　　　　　　) will rise from almost one in four to one in three. The Japanese government has spent too much money on costly and meaningless (　　　　　　) projects and not enough on growing the country's population. Japanese couples rarely have more than two children. Personal incomes are not growing, parents are having children later, and there is a lack of child-care (　　　　　　). Three things are necessary to promote a higher birth rate. First, the government must provide more (　　　　　　) day-care centers. Second, companies should do more to promote younger workers and reduce overtime work. Third, the government should encourage more women to enter the labor (　　　　　　) at a high level and return to work after childbirth.

4 CDをもう一度聴いてシャドーイングしてみよう。

COLUMN

　少子化対策として時の政権は様々な取組みをしてきた。合計特殊出生率が丙午の1966年の水準を下回った1990年の1.57ショックが契機となり、国は出生率低下と子どもの数の減少を日本の大問題と認識して対策をたててきた。1994年にはエンゼルプランと緊急保育対策等5カ年事業、1999年に新エンゼルプラン、2001年に保育園の待機児童ゼロ作戦、これらは保育サービスを中心としたものである。効果は目に見える形で上がらず、民主党が政権を取ってから2011年には「子ども手当」として子供一人に一律16,000円が支給され、高校の授業料無償化も行なわれた。

　第2次安倍政権では児童手当と高校無償化は所得制限を設けて続けられている。これらに対し国債を膨張させるお金のバラマキとの批判もある。政党や首長の選挙公約や政策ブレーンは託児所・保育施設の充実を必ず提唱するが、待機児童をゼロにすることはなかなかできない。その一方、自宅で介護が必要な親の面倒を見ている家族のための「託老所」なるものが現れた。

UNIT 4
Safe Food for Japan
アメリカが注目する日本の食品安全基準

By MARTIN FACKLER   October 11, 2007

中国製毒入り餃子事件がきっかけとなり輸入食品の安全性が心配されている。食料自給率がきわめて低い日本は、外国からの食品輸入に頼らざるをえないので、安全性の確保をめざして様々な努力をしてきた。アメリカは日本のどのような取り組みをまねようとしているか。

KEYWORDS
🎧 1 - 26, 27

A. 記事読解に特に重要な語句の意味を確認しよう。

1. rigorous   2. merchandise

3. spinach   4. regulate

5. contaminated   6. draconian

7. antibiotics   8. incentive

9. unscrupulous   10. conscientious

B. 上下の語群で意味の近いものを結び付け、記事に現れる難易度の高い語句の言い換えを確認しよう。

1. concerned (　)   2. ship   (　)   3. issue   (　)
4. consumers (　)   5. publicized (　)   6. hazardous (　)
7. uproar   (　)   8. stringent (　)   9. banned   (　)
10. enforce   (　)

a. export	b. buyers	c. carry out	d. dangerous
e. strict	f. confusion	g. announced	h. release
i. forbidden	j. anxious		

19

1 TOKYO, Oct. 10—With Americans growing increasingly concerned about the safety of Chinese products, Washington has begun looking for solutions in Japan. The Japanese have developed tough approaches for ensuring the quality of Chinese imports, particularly food—in part by far more **rigorous** testing of its imported food than in the United States. But the innovation getting the most American attention is Japan's system for screening Chinese producers even before they ship their **merchandise** to Japan.

2 A report released last week by the House Energy and Commerce Committee cited Japan's system for monitoring **spinach** and other Chinese food exports as a possible model for importers in the United States. Last month, a White House working group issued its own report after visiting Tokyo, and even Chinese officials have urged the United States to adopt the Japanese approach.

3 Citing the Food and Drug Administration, the House report described Japan's model as the most realistic one for protecting American consumers. "The Japanese system of **regulating** Chinese food imports does appear to offer better control than that currently used by F.D.A.," it concluded.

4 The program is the product of Japan's longer experience with Chinese safety problems, going back to the discovery five years ago of high levels of pesticide in Chinese frozen spinach. Americans have become more conscious of such safety issues this year, with the highly publicized recalls of Chinese-made toys **contaminated** with lead paint and pet food ingredients containing hazardous chemicals. "Japan is five years ahead of the rest of the world in dealing with quality problems from China," said Tatsuya Kakita, the author of several books here on food safety. "The world can learn from Japan."

5 Japan, which buys far more of its food from China than the United States does, has focused its efforts so far on food safety. But some Japanese and American officials and safety experts say that similar methods may also work for many Chinese exports to the United States, not only seafood and processed vegetables but also products like medicine, toys and paint.

6 It is rare for American officials to praise Japanese import controls. Washington more often criticizes Japan's regulations as **draconian**, especially when applied to American products. Indeed, one of the top trade disputes in recent years between the two countries has been over Japanese limits on American beef imports, after the discovery in 2003 of a case of mad cow disease in the United

States.

7 Food safety is a particularly delicate issue in Japan, which imports 60 percent of its food supply. After the problems with Chinese-grown spinach created an uproar here in 2002, the government stepped up random testing of all imported food. The Japanese health ministry says it and private laboratories now test samples from about 10 percent of all food shipments entering the country. By contrast, the United States, which imports about a tenth of its food, tests less than 1 percent of shipments, according to the House report.

8 Many of Japan's stringent tests take place at two national inspection centers. On a recent morning at the center in the port of Yokohama, agents in white lab coats examined more than 100 samples—grinding up lemons, asparagus and even turtle meat in large industrial blenders to test them for banned pesticides, **antibiotics** and other chemicals. The Yokohama center alone tested more than 30,000 samples last year, about three times what the United States tested. "We are the front line in protecting consumers," said Yukihiro Shiomi, an inspector at the center.

9 The health ministry says Japan tested 203,001 samples of food last year and found 1,515 samples that violated standards. The largest number of violations, a third, came from China, which supplies about 15 percent of Japan's food imports.

10 While there have been calls in Washington for stepped-up testing, there is also notable interest in Japan's new system for screening Chinese producers. Introduced last year, the system is used only for spinach. But the program has been so successful in eliminating quality problems that Tokyo plans to expand it to other types of food imports, said Kazuhiko Tsurumi, deputy director of the health ministry's import food safety office. "The lesson from our success with improving the safety of spinach is that direct control of producers is the best method for quality control," he said.

11 Under the system, a number of Chinese companies receive licenses from the government there allowing them to export to Japan on the condition that they maintain Japanese standards. Currently, 45 Chinese companies are licensed to produce spinach for sale in Japan. The Chinese producers must grow all their spinach on their own plots and not buy any from other producers. This greatly reduces the chance of dangerous pesticides getting into shipments, Japanese

officials say.

12 While China has licensed exporters before, this system is more stringent, Japanese and American officials say, in part because the health ministry helps to <u>enforce</u> it by allowing in products only from licensed companies. By contrast, the United States, with its free-market approach, allows importers to disregard China's licensing system.

13 Japanese officials acknowledge that their system limits competition, allowing Chinese producers to charge the Japanese consumer higher prices. But they say that this profit **incentive** also keeps the Chinese companies adhering to Japanese standards—lest they lose their licenses. Tokyo also requires Japanese importers to test every shipment of spinach for banned pesticides and other chemicals.

14 The mandatory testing adds about $160 in costs to each shipment, the health ministry says. Spinach now costs about $4 a pound in suburban Tokyo, two to two and a half times what an American might pay, though most of that difference results from other factors, like Japan's archaic distribution system. But the Japanese say that the controls solve a big challenge in importing from China: weeding out **unscrupulous** producers, without hurting China's many **conscientious** ones. Yet, at a Summit supermarket in the Tokyo suburb of Mitaka, such steps have done little to alleviate fears of Chinese quality problems, which have received intense media coverage here.

15 Sales of Chinese-grown produce are a tenth of what they were just five years ago, as consumers embrace pricier Japanese products. The sense of security in domestic fruit and vegetables is enhanced by the store's practice of posting the names, addresses and even photos of local farmers who grow the produce. "I prefer the farmers' faces," said Yumiko Ishihara, a 38-year-old homemaker. "Buying Chinese is like gambling with my family's health." (1070 words)

Unit 4　Safe Food for Japan

NOTES

l.2　Washington　各国の首都名が擬人化されて「～国政府」の意味で用いられるのはニュース英語において顕著な用法。この記事では他にどこに見えるだろうか。

l.18　pesticide　「殺虫剤」「除草剤」は herbicide, weed killer、「農薬」は一般に agrichemicals [agro-]。「残留農薬」は agrichemical residues。

l.23　Tatsuya Kakita　「垣田達哉氏」消費者問題研究所代表で、生鮮食品の実態や自給率問題、健康食品などの加工食品、食品表示偽装問題などの第一人者。『もうだまされない食品表示—身近な法律』（1998、三水社）、『ホントは怖い！加工食品の真実—食卓に並ぶ食品、本当に口にして大丈夫？』（2013、英和出版社）、『あなたも食べてる中国産』（2007、リヨン社）など著書は多数。この文の here は、第7段落の here と同様、日本を指すようだ。

l.34　mad cow disease　「狂牛病」正式名は bovine spongiform encephalopathy (BSE)。1986年に英国で最初の狂牛病が発生し1990年から1991年に最大発生を見た。日本でも2000年以降に30頭以上の感染牛が発見されたが、餌の規制によって2003年以降に出生した牛からは感染は出ていない。

ll.59-60　the health ministry's import food safety office　「厚生労働省、医薬食品局食品安全部監視安全課、輸入食品安全対策室」室長は2013年現在道野英司氏。

l.90　produce　動詞 produce から派生された名詞は2つあり、product は工業製品に、produce は主に農産物に用いられる。

l.94　homemaker　「主婦」の意味で（家に閉じこもっていることを匂わす）housewife に代わって用いられるようになった。-maker の形式の語には policymaker「政治家」、holiday-maker「旅行客」、kingmaker「政党の実力者」、lawmaker「立法者」、lossmaker「赤字産業」、peacemaker「仲裁人」などがある。

EXERCISES

1　本文に基づいて以下の問いに英語で答えなさい。

1. What is attracting the attention of most Americans concerning imported Chinese food?

2. What kind of condition do Chinese companies meet in order to get the license from the local government to export spinach to Japan?

3. Why have Tokyo and Washington been disputing over Japanese limits on American beef imports?

2 本文に基づいて以下の問いに答えなさい。

1. アメリカ人が中国からの輸入食品の安全性を気に掛けるようになった理由は何ですか。

   _____
   _____
   _____

2. 本記事では日本の輸入食品の検査基準が厳しいことを「厳しい」の意味の類語の言い換えで強調しています。それらの類語を抜き出しなさい。

   _____
   _____
   _____

3. 第13段落の表現 "this profit incentive" について説明しなさい。

   _____
   _____
   _____

3 CDを聴いて以下の要約文の空欄に適語を入れなさい。　　1 - 34

Concerned about the safety of imports from China, the US is looking at the way Japan (　　　　　　　) screens imports from that country. Japan tests many food samples in national inspection centers. Japan now has a new system for (　　　　　　　　　) spinach producers in China. Japan gives licenses to 45 Chinese companies allowing them to export to Japan on the (　　　　　　　) that they maintain Japanese standards. They must grow all their spinach on their own plots and not buy any from other producers. In (　　　　　　　), the US takes a free-market approach. The controls make the spinach more expensive, but the government says they solve a big problem in importing from China by weeding out (　　　　　　　　) producers and rewarding conscientious ones. Japanese consumers, however, are still concerned about Chinese produce.

4 CDをもう一度聴いてシャドーイングしてみよう。　　1 - 34

UNIT 5: Timing a Rise in Sea Level

極地の氷が解ければ海面上昇

By JUSTIN GILLIS　　　August 12, 2013

温暖化は予想を超えて急速に進んでおり、日本でも40度を越える酷暑やゲリラ豪雨、春から上陸する台風など亜熱帯になったような気がする。しかし温暖化の影響が顕著に表れているのは北極と南極だ。極地の氷が解けると海面はどのくらい上昇するのか。それはいつ起きるのか。

KEYWORDS　　　CD 1 - 35, 36

A. 記事読解に特に重要な語句の意味を確認しよう。

1. emissions
2. Greenhouse Effect
3. geologic time scale
4. intriguing
5. vindication
6. nail
7. hold up
8. catastrophic
9. augur
10. threshold

B. 上下の語群で意味の近いものを結び付け、記事に現れる難易度の高い語句の言い換えを確認しよう。

1. consequences　（　）　2. topography　（　）　3. degrade　（　）
4. instability　（　）　5. colleague　（　）　6. stabilize　（　）
7. compelling　（　）　8. disclose　（　）　9. implication　（　）
10. crucial　（　）

a. become worse　　b. make something unlikely to change
c. fellow worker　　d. reveal　　e. convincing　　f. suggestion
g. results　　h. arrangements of the natural features of an area
i. deciding　　j. uncertainty

25

[1] Thirty-five years ago, a scientist named John H. Mercer issued a warning. By then it was already becoming clear that human **emissions** would warm the earth, and Dr. Mercer had begun thinking deeply about the consequences. His paper, in the journal *Nature*, was titled "West Antarctic Ice Sheet and CO2 **Greenhouse Effect**: A Threat of Disaster." In it, Dr. Mercer pointed out the unusual topography of the ice sheet sitting over the western part of Antarctica. Much of it is below sea level, in a sort of bowl, and he said that a climatic warming could cause the whole thing to degrade rapidly on a **geologic time scale**, leading to a possible rise in sea level of 16 feet.

[2] While it is clear by now that we are in the early stages of what is likely to be a substantial rise in sea level, we still do not know if Dr. Mercer was right about a dangerous instability that could cause that rise to happen rapidly, in geologic time. We may be getting closer to figuring that out.

[3] An **intriguing** new paper comes from Michael J. O'Leary of Curtin University in Australia and five colleagues scattered around the world. Dr. O'Leary has spent more than a decade exploring the remote western coast of Australia, considered one of the best places in the world to study sea levels of the past. The paper, published July 28 in *Nature Geoscience*, focuses on a warm period in the earth's history that preceded the most recent ice age. In that epoch, sometimes called the Eemian, the planetary temperature was similar to levels we may see in coming decades as a result of human emissions, so it is considered a possible indicator of things to come.

[4] Examining elevated fossil beaches and coral reefs along more than a thousand miles of coast, Dr. O'Leary's group confirmed something we pretty much already knew. In the warmer world of the Eemian, sea level stabilized for several thousand years at about 10 to 12 feet above modern sea level.

[5] The interesting part is what happened after that. Dr. O'Leary's group found what they consider to be compelling evidence that near the end of the Eemian, sea level jumped by another 17 feet or so, to settle at close to 30 feet above the modern level, before beginning to fall as the ice age set in. In an interview, Dr. O'Leary told me he was confident that the 17-foot jump happened in less than a thousand years—how much less, he cannot be sure.

[6] This finding is something of a **vindication** for one member of the team, a North Carolina field geologist, Paul J. Hearty. He had argued for decades that the

rock record suggested a jump of this sort, but only recently have measurement and modeling techniques reached the level of precision needed to **nail** the case.

[7] We have to see if their results withstand critical scrutiny. A sea-level scientist not involved in the work, Andrea Dutton of the University of Florida, said the paper had failed to <u>disclose</u> enough detailed information about the field sites to allow her to judge the overall conclusion. But if the work does **hold up**, the <u>implications</u> are profound. The only possible explanation for such a large, rapid jump in sea level is the **catastrophic** collapse of a polar ice sheet, on either Greenland or Antarctica.

[8] Dr. O'Leary is not prepared to say which; figuring that out is the group's next project. But a 17-foot rise in less than a thousand years, a geologic instant, has to mean that one or both ice sheets contain some instability that can be set off by a warmer climate. That, of course, **augurs** poorly for humans. Scientists at Stanford calculated recently that human emissions are causing the climate to change many times faster than at any point since the dinosaurs died out. We are pushing the climate system so hard that, if the ice sheets do have a **threshold** of some kind, we stand a good chance of exceeding it.

[9] Another recent paper, by Anders Levermann of the Potsdam Institute for Climate Impact Research in Germany and a half-dozen colleagues, implies that even if emissions were to stop tomorrow, we have probably locked in several feet of sea level rise over the long term. Benjamin Strauss and his colleagues at Climate Central, an independent group of scientists and journalists in Princeton that reports climate research, translated the Levermann results into graphical form, and showed the difference it could make if we launched an aggressive program to control emissions. By 2100, their calculations suggest, continuing on our current path would mean locking in a long-term sea level rise of 23 feet, but aggressive emission cuts could limit that to seven feet.

[10] If you are the mayor of Miami or of a beach town in New Jersey, you may be asking yourself: Exactly how long is all this going to take to play out? On that <u>crucial</u> point, alas, our science is still nearly blind. Scientists can look at the rocks and see indisputable evidence of jumps in sea level, and they can associate those with relatively modest increases in global temperature. But the nature of the evidence is such that it is hard to tell the difference between something that happened in a thousand years and something that happened in a hundred.

11 On the human time scale, of course, that is all the difference in the world. If sea level is going to rise by, say, 30 feet over several thousand years, that is quite a lot of time to adjust—to pull back from the beaches, to reinforce major cities, and to develop technologies to help us cope. But if sea level is capable of rising several feet per century, as Dr. O'Leary's paper would seem to imply and as many other scientists believe, then babies being born now could live to see the early stages of a global calamity. (994 words)

NOTES

l.2 human emissions　環境問題を論じる英文にはこの省略表現が頻出するが、もちろん「人による排出」という表現にはgreenhouse gases「温暖化ガス」、特に「二酸化炭素」carbon dioxideが含意されている。Unit 2, l.41で既出、本記事の第3段落と次の記事の第2段落にも出るので注意。

l.4 West Antarctic　南極大陸は東側は半球形の陸地でこの海岸線に沿って南極圏（南緯66．33以南）が設定されているが、西側には南極半島と呼ばれる突出部があり、その付け根にウェッデル海、その反対側のロス海と呼ばれる大きな湾があって陸地が少ない。この海上の氷棚が不安定になっており少なくなっている。

l.4 ice sheet　「氷床」地面の上に積もった氷のこと。海面に張り出した氷の塊はice shelf「氷棚（ひょうほう）」、その端が崩れて海上を浮遊しているのがiceberg「氷山」である。

l.20 Eemian　「エーム間氷期」英語表記はEemian interglacial periodである。12万5千年前の最後の間氷期。

ll.41-42 a large, rapid jump　名詞に2個の形容詞が付く場合、3種の並び方がある。"a handsome old man"や"angry young men"のように形容詞の種類が異なる時は、本質的性質や不変の状態を表す形容詞ほど後ろに置かれて連続するが、並列する状態や対抗する性質などはandで結ばれる。この例のようにコンマで繋がれているのはポーズがあることを示し、andで繋がれているのと等しい。ちなみにニュース英語の見出し（Title, Headline）ではandの代わりにコンマを置くことが多い（例：China, South Korea face familiar woes in English quest「中国と韓国も（日本と同様）英語教育がうまくいかず苦しんでいる」）。Unit 1, l.33の"in slow, quiet Japanese"参照。

ll.45-46 has to mean　この"has to mean"は"we have to understand, we must be sure"のように言い換えたらわかりやすいだろう。

l.54 even if emissions were to stop tomorrow　ハワイマウナロア山の測候所の観測では1960年から2013年にかけて二酸化炭素の大気中濃度は315PPM前後から395PPM前後に増えている。

l.54 locked in　"lock in"は「鍵を掛けて閉じ込める」が原義で、ここでは「閉じ込める、おさえる」または、「（予想される悪い結果を）動かせなくなる、何の対処も出来なくなる」のような意であろう。

l.63 play out　"play out"は、ここでは「最後まで演奏する、使い切る」ではなく、「（実際に事が）起きる、（筋書きを）実演する」に似た用法であるから、「この理論が実現する」のような意味であろう。

Unit 5 Timing a Rise in Sea Level

EXERCISES

1 本文に基づいて以下の問いに英語で答えなさい。

1. What did Dr. Mercer predict thirty-five years ago?

2. Which place is considered one of the best places in the world to study sea levels of the past?

3. What is that which climate scientists cannot tell about the past sea level rise?

2 本文に基づいて以下の問いに答えなさい。

1. 第1段落に見られる表現 geologic time scale と対比的に用いられている表現は何ですか。それぞれどのくらいの期間を指しているでしょうか。

2. オーストラリアの西海岸地域が過去の海面の高さの変化を調べるのに適しているのはなぜでしょうか。

3. O'Leary 博士らの研究が正しいとすると、イーム紀の終わりの千年以内に海面が17フィートも上昇した原因は何だと考えられますか。

3 CDを聴いて以下の要約文の空欄に適語を入れなさい。

One scientist warned that the melting of the West Antarctic Ice Sheet could lead to a 16-foot rise in sea levels. An Australian researcher has studied the Eemian Period, which (　　　　　) just before the last Ice Age. Temperatures then were similar to those that may be caused by (　　　　　) warming. In less than a thousand years, sea levels jumped about 17 feet toward the end of this period. One possible (　　　　　) is the melting of a giant ice sheet either in Greenland or Antarctica. A German researcher recently stated that even if greenhouse gas (　　　　　) stop tomorrow, this will not prevent sea levels from rising. His research suggests that if we introduce (　　　　　) cuts, we can bring down this rise from 23 feet to 7 feet.

4 CDをもう一度聴いてシャドーイングしてみよう。

COLUMN

　2009年の夏にアメリカ東海岸では海面が想定より約60センチ上昇し、周期的変動パターンを予測していた気象学者が驚いた。当局の報告によれば、直接の原因は地球温暖化とは別のメキシコ湾流の弱体化と大西洋北東部からの安定した風であると判明したが、根本的原因はわかっていない。科学者たちは、グリーンランドの氷床が崩壊すると淡水が海に流れ込んで大西洋の海水循環パターンが乱れて、海水の体積が増えて海面上昇が起きると考えている。以前の研究では、氷床が今のペースで解け続けると、今世紀中にニューヨーク市周辺の海面は他の地域と比べて2倍も上昇すると予想していた。

最近の研究では、グリーンランド氷床が今のペースで解け続けると、ニューヨークやマイアミを含む1,700を超えるアメリカの都市や街が、今世紀中に海面より低くなるという。

　温暖化による海面上昇問題のシンボルになっているのは洋上の島国である。ツバルはオセアニア南太平洋エリス諸島の海抜5メートル以下の島国である。首都フナフティに関西電力が2007年からの工事で太陽光発電設備を設置、50世帯分の電力が賄えるようになった。1,000以上の島からなるインド洋のモルジブはその8割が海抜1.5メートル以下で、ほとんどすべての島で海岸浸食が進んでいる。

UNIT 6

What to Make of a Warming Plateau

最近10年は温暖化の停滞期？

By JUSTIN GILLIS　　　　　　　　　　　　　　　　　June 10, 2013

二酸化炭素の排出量が増えているのに、最近15年程は平均気温が上昇していない。温暖化は終わったのか、停滞しているだけなのか。停滞しているとすれば、その原因をさぐることで、温暖化を遅らせ、ふせぐことができはしないか。科学者たちの様々な見解を学ぼう。

KEYWORDS

1 - 43, 44

A. 記事読解に特に重要な語句の意味を確認しよう。

1. luck out　　　　　　　　2. lull

3. in fits and starts　　　　4. investment

5. futility　　　　　　　　　6. cherry-pick

7. statisticians　　　　　　8. suspect (n.)

9. proffer　　　　　　　　10. halcyon days

B. 上下の語群で意味の近いものを結び付け、記事に現れる難易度の高い語句の言い換えを確認しよう。

1. accumulate　　(　)　　2. variability　　(　)　　3. dismissive　　(　)
4. make much of　(　)　　5. staggering　　(　)　　6. trap　　　　　(　)
7. pollution　　　(　)　　8. circulation　　(　)　　9. ultimately　　(　)
10. prologue　　　(　)

a. rejecting　　　b. emphasize　　　c. build up　　　d. uncleanness
e. streams of water　f. changeability　g. introduction　h. surprising
i. finally　　　　j. catch

1 As unlikely as this may sound, we have **lucked out** in recent years when it comes to global warming. The rise in the surface temperature of earth has been markedly slower over the last 15 years than in the 20 years before that. And that **lull** in warming has occurred even as greenhouse gases have accumulated in the atmosphere at a record pace.

2 The slowdown is a bit of a mystery to climate scientists. True, the basic theory that predicts a warming of the planet in response to human emissions does not suggest that warming should be smooth and continuous. To the contrary, in a climate system still dominated by natural variability, there is every reason to think the warming will proceed **in fits and starts**.

3 But given how much is riding on the scientific forecast, the practitioners of climate science would like to understand exactly what is going on. They admit that they do not, even though some potential mechanisms of the slowdown have been suggested. The situation highlights important gaps in our knowledge of the climate system, some of which cannot be closed until we get better measurements from high in space and from deep in the ocean.

4 As you might imagine, those dismissive of climate-change concerns have made much of this warming plateau. They typically argue that "global warming stopped 15 years ago" or some similar statement, and then assert that this disproves the whole notion that greenhouse gases are causing warming. Rarely do they mention that most of the warmest years in the historical record have occurred recently. Moreover, their claim depends on careful selection of the starting and ending points. The starting point is almost always 1998, a particularly warm year because of a strong El Niño weather pattern.

5 Somebody who wanted to sell you gold coins as an **investment** could make the same kind of argument about the **futility** of putting your retirement funds into the stock market. If he picked the start date and the end date carefully enough, the gold salesman could make it look like the stock market did not go up for a decade or longer. But that does not really tell you what your retirement money is going to do in the market over 30 or 40 years. It does not even tell you how you would have done over the **cherry-picked** decade, which would have depended on exactly when you got in and out of the market.

6 Scientists and **statisticians** reject this sort of selective use of numbers, and when they calculate the long-term temperature trends for the earth, they

conclude that it continues to warm through time. Despite the recent lull, it is an open question whether the pace of that warming has undergone any lasting shift. What to make of it all?

[7] We certainly cannot conclude, as some people want to, that carbon dioxide is not actually a greenhouse gas. More than a century of research thoroughly disproves that claim. In fact, scientists can calculate how much extra heat should be accumulating from the human-caused increases in greenhouse gases, and the energies involved are <u>staggering</u>. By a conservative estimate, current concentrations are <u>trapping</u> an extra amount of energy equivalent to 400,000 Hiroshima bombs exploding across the face of the earth every day.

[8] So the real question is where all that heat is going, if not to warm the surface. And a prime **suspect** is the deep ocean. Our measurements there are not good enough to confirm it absolutely, but a growing body of research suggests this may be an important part of the answer. Exactly why the ocean would have started to draw down extra heat in recent years is a mystery, and one we badly need to understand. But the main ideas have to do with possible shifts in winds and currents that are causing surface heat to be pulled down faster than before.

[9] The deep-ocean theory is one of a half-dozen explanations that have been **proffered** for the warming plateau. Perhaps the answer will turn out to be some mix of all of them. And in any event, computer forecasts of climate change suggest that pauses in warming lasting a couple of decades should not surprise us.

[10] Now, here is a crucial piece of background: it turns out we had an earlier plateau in global warming, from roughly the 1950s to the 1970s, and scientists do not fully understand that one either. A lot of evidence suggests that sunlight-blocking <u>pollution</u> from dirty factories may have played a role, as did natural variability in ocean <u>circulation</u>. The pollution was <u>ultimately</u> reduced by stronger clean-air laws in the West. Today, factory pollution from China and other developing countries could be playing a similar role in blocking some sunlight. We will not know for sure until we send up satellites that can make better measurements of particles in the air.

[11] What happened when the mid-20th-century lull came to an end? You guessed it: an extremely rapid warming of the planet. So, if past is <u>prologue</u>, this current plateau will end at some point, too, and a new era of rapid global warming

will begin. That will put extra energy and moisture into the atmosphere that can fuel weather extremes, like heat waves and torrential rains. We might one day find ourselves looking back on the crazy weather of the 2010s with a deep yearning for those **halcyon days**. (901 words)

NOTES

タイトル What to make of このタイトルはわかりづらいが "make much/little of …"「重要視する／軽んずる」という表現に基づいており、「温暖化の停滞は重要なことだろうか」「最近の温暖化停滞の受け取り方」のような意味になる。第4段落のはじめの文を参照。第6段落の終わりに再出。

l.5 at a record pace 国連世界気象機構（World Meteorological Organization 略WMO、本部ジュネーブ）の統計によれば世界の年間平均気温は1850年代から1910年代まで13.7度前後で安定していた。1920年代から40年代に14.1度に上昇、その後は1980年まで約40年間は14度前後で安定していたが、その後の20年間で14.5度まで急上昇し、21世紀に入ってから10年程は14.3〜14.5度で安定している。

l.10 in fits and starts この熟語はUnit 14の最終段落で再出。

l.11 riding on "ride on" は「〜に依る、〜次第である」または「〜に乗って運ばれる」のように取れば解釈可能。

l.15 closed "closed" は前の行の gaps が意味上の目的語。名詞 gap は "to bridge the East-West cultural gap"「西洋と東洋の文化の溝を埋める」、"His finding filled a gap in our knowledge of the evolution of men."「彼の発見で人類の進化の知識の欠落が埋まった」、"[How] Can we narrow the gap?"「どうすれば溝を埋めることができるか」（決まり文句）のような動詞と共起する。

l.17 those "those who are dismissive of" の短縮形で「〜のような人々＝科学者」の意味。

l.24 El Niño El Niñoはスペイン語「息子＝幼子イエス」、クリスマスの時期にこの現象が起きることからの命名。赤道域の太平洋で数年おきに発生する海面温度上昇現象で、異常気象を世界に引き起こす原因と考えられている。女性形La Niña「娘」は海面温度低下現象を指す。

l.44 Hiroshima bombs 1945年8月6日に広島に投下された原子爆弾は、核分裂物質約1キログラムが分裂、TNT火薬2万トン相当の爆発エネルギーを発した。これは2×10^{13}calのエネルギーである。

Unit 6 What to Make of a Warming Plateau

EXERCISES

1 本文に基づいて以下の問いに英語で答えなさい。

1. What is the deep-ocean theory?

2. What is the typical greenhouse gas? (Name one typical greenhouse gas.)

3. When did we have an earlier plateau in global warming?

2 本文に基づいて以下の問いに答えなさい。

1. 最近の気温上昇の停滞現象について科学者の間では二つの異なる見解があります。それを説明しなさい。

2. 最近の気温上昇の停滞の原因として「深海説」以外にどのようなものが考えられますか。

3. この記事では「温暖化の一時停止」について考察しているので「休止・停滞」の意味の類語が多く用いられています。それらを抜き出して比較しましょう。

3 CDを聴いて以下の要約文の空欄に適語を入れなさい。

The rise in the surface temperature of earth has slowed over the last 15 years even though greenhouse gases have rapidly (   ) in the atmosphere. Scientists do not know why, but it is possible to calculate that current (   ) of greenhouse gases are trapping a huge amount of energy every day. Among various explanations is one theory that suggests this heat is being drawn down into the deep ocean possibly because of shifts in winds and (   ). Computer forecasts of climate change suggest that pauses in warming lasting a couple of (   ) are not surprising. In fact, from roughly the 1950s to the 1970s, there was an earlier plateau in global warming, which scientists do not fully understand. It therefore seems likely that this current (   ) will also end at some point.

4 CDをもう一度聴いてシャドーイングしてみよう。

COLUMN

　西暦4～5世紀のゲルマン民族の大移動は、寒冷化が原因であるという説がある。その後の西暦800～1300年頃は全地球的に現在並みの温暖な時期で、ノルマン人が大西洋を渡って（名前の通りの）グリーンランドに入植し、アイスランドでも麦類の栽培が可能であった。これを中世温暖期と呼ぶ。その後14世紀半ばから19世紀半ばに渡って小氷期と呼ばれる寒冷化が見られた。アルプスの氷河は拡大してふもとの村を飲み込み、テムズ川やオランダの運河や港湾が氷結した。

　この2000年ほどの間には数百年ごとに温暖期と寒冷期が交代してきたのであり、歴史上大戦乱が続いた時期はこの寒冷期に当たり、食糧不足がその主な原因とも考えられるのである。寒冷期には陸上の氷床が増えて海面が下降して現在の島嶼部も陸続きになっていた。渡れなかった大河も氷結するので民族の大移動も可能であったという。

UNIT 7 The Decline of E-Empires

IT帝国の落日

By PAUL KRUGMAN

August 25, 2013

現代IT業界の覇権争いと古代北アフリカ王朝の栄枯盛衰。一見無縁の両者に共通の原理が働いているようだと、著名な経済学者ポール・クルーグマンは指摘する。描かれる複雑な人間心理を読み取ろう。

KEYWORDS

1 - 51, 52

A. 記事読解に特に重要な語句の意味を確認しよう。

1. e-empire
2. network externality
3. antitrust enforcement
4. operating system
5. premium price
6. market share
7. rise and fall of dynasties
8. barbarian
9. monopoly rent
10. creative destruction

B. 上下の語群で意味の近いものを結び付け、記事に現れる難易度の高い語句の言い換えを確認しよう。

1. geek   ( )   2. guru   ( )   3. upheaval   ( )
4. legend   ( )   5. futile   ( )   6. dominate   ( )
7. complacent   ( )   8. case   ( )   9. extract   ( )
10. inhibit   ( )

a. chieftain	b. shake-up	c. restrain	d. remove
e. plea	f. self-satisfied	g. conquer	h. faithful
i. caption	j. useless		

[1] Steve Ballmer's surprise announcement that he will be resigning as Microsoft's C.E.O. has set off a huge flood of commentary. Being neither a tech geek nor a management guru, I can't add much on those fronts. I do, however, think I know a bit about economics, and I also read a lot of history. So the Ballmer announcement has me thinking about **network externalities** and Ibn Khaldun. And thinking about these things, I'd argue, can help ensure that we draw the right lessons from this particular corporate upheaval.

[2] First, about network externalities: Consider the state of the computer industry circa 2000, when Microsoft's share price hit its peak and the company seemed utterly dominant. Remember the T-shirts depicting Bill Gates as a Borg (part of the hive mind from "Star Trek"), with the legend, "Resistance is futile. Prepare to be assimilated"? Remember when Microsoft was at the center of concerns about **antitrust enforcement**?

[3] The odd thing was that nobody seemed to like Microsoft's products. By all accounts, Apple computers were better than PCs using Windows as their **operating system**. Yet the vast majority of desktop and laptop computers ran Windows. Why?

[4] The answer, basically, is that everyone used Windows because everyone used Windows. If you had a Windows PC and wanted help, you could ask the guy in the next cubicle, or the tech people downstairs, and have a very good chance of getting the answer you needed. Software was designed to run on PCs; peripheral devices were designed to work with PCs.

[5] That's network externalities in action, and it made Microsoft a monopolist. The story of how that state of affairs arose is tangled, but I don't think it's too unfair to say that Apple mistakenly believed that ordinary buyers would value its superior quality as much as its own people did. So it charged **premium prices**, and by the time it realized how many people were choosing cheaper machines that weren't insanely great but did the job, Microsoft's dominance was locked in.

[6] Now, any such discussion brings out the Apple faithful, who insist that anything Windows can do Apple can do better and that only idiots buy PCs. They may be right. But it doesn't matter, because there are many such idiots, myself included. And Windows still dominates the personal computer market.

[7] The trouble for Microsoft came with the rise of new devices whose importance

it famously failed to grasp. "There's no chance," declared Mr. Ballmer in 2007, "that the iPhone is going to get any significant **market share**."

8 How could Microsoft have been so blind? Here's where Ibn Khaldun comes in. He was a 14th-century Islamic philosopher who basically invented what we would now call the social sciences. And one insight he had, based on the history of his native North Africa, was that there was a rhythm to the **rise and fall of dynasties**.

9 Desert tribesmen, he argued, always have more courage and social cohesion than settled, civilized folk, so every once in a while they will sweep in and conquer lands whose rulers have become corrupt and complacent. They create a new dynasty — and, over time, become corrupt and complacent themselves, ready to be overrun by a new set of **barbarians**.

10 I don't think it's much of a stretch to apply this story to Microsoft, a company that did so well with its operating-system monopoly that it lost focus, while Apple — still wandering in the wilderness after all those years — was alert to new opportunities. And so the barbarians swept in from the desert.

11 Sometimes, by the way, barbarians are invited in by a domestic faction seeking a shake-up. This may be what's happening at Yahoo: Marissa Mayer doesn't look much like a fierce Bedouin chieftain, but she's arguably filling the same functional role.

12 Anyway, the funny thing is that Apple's position in mobile devices now bears a strong resemblance to Microsoft's former position in operating systems. True, Apple produces high-quality products. But they are, by most accounts, little if any better than those of rivals, while selling at premium prices.

13 So why do people buy them? Network externalities: lots of other people use iWhatevers, there are more apps for iOS than for other systems, so Apple becomes the safe and easy choice. Meet the new boss, same as the old boss.

14 Is there a policy moral here? Let me make at least a negative case: Even though Microsoft did not, in fact, end up taking over the world, those antitrust concerns weren't misplaced. Microsoft was a monopolist, it did extract a lot of **monopoly rents**, and it did inhibit innovation. **Creative destruction** means that monopolies aren't forever, but it doesn't mean that they're harmless while they last. This was true for Microsoft yesterday; it may be true for Apple, or Google, or someone not yet on our radar, tomorrow. (805 words)

NOTES

Paul Krugman　「ポール・クルーグマン」プリンストン大学教授。2008年ノーベル経済学賞受賞。New York Timesで1999年からOp-Edでコラムを担当している。本記事はその一つ。代表的著作に『そして日本経済が世界の希望になる』（2013 山形浩生・大野和基訳、PHP研究所）、『さっさと不況を終わらせろ』（2012 山形浩生訳、早川書房）など。なお、Op-Edはopposite editorialの略で、社説欄（editorial）の反対側（opposite）の特別ページのこと。署名入りの評論がよく掲載される。Krugmanについては本ユニットのコラムも参照。

l.3 management guru　マネジメントの世界で影響力の極めて強い人物はguruと呼ばれる。なお、このような人物を称えるGlobal Management Guru Awardという賞がある。その趣旨は同賞公式サイト（http://www.globalmanagementguru.org/）によれば以下の通り。"Global Management Guru Award is conferred on a scholar and a Thought Leader in Management, present or past, who has influenced management thought worldwide in a fundamental way as a teacher, researcher, writer and a mentor."

l.11 the hive mind　「ハイブマインド」蜂の群れ（hive）のように、個体を超えて、集団として機能する知能（mind）のこと。ここで言及されているStar TrekのBorgはその一例。

l.18 basically　文全体を修飾する要素が文中に置かれる場合、このように文の第二要素となることが多い。他に同様の語順が見られる文を本記事中で見つけてみよう。

l.42 more courage and social cohesion　courageとcohesionが同じく/k/で始まり、頭韻（alliteration）を踏んでいる。この段落に二度現れるcorrupt and complacentも頭韻句、さらには、この段落の重要な動詞であるconquerとcreateも語頭音が/k/である。結果、全体としてリズムがよく、音読に心地よい一節となっている。頭韻は様々な日常的な表現によく用いられている。探してみよう。

l.49 wandering in the wilderness　『民数記』第14章33節からの引用。in the wildernessは、政治家が「下野（失脚）して」の意で使われることもある。

l.52 Marissa Mayer　「マリッサ・メイヤー」アメリカYahoo!の社長兼CEO。2012年から現職でそれまではGoogle社の幹部であり、G-mail等の主要サービスの開発設計に関わっていた。Google社初の女性エンジニアである。

ll.55-56 bears a strong resemblance　resemblanceはshowやhave以外にこの箇所のようにbearとよく共起する。

l.60 iWhatevers　iPS細胞のiがアップル製品のiと無関係でないことはよく知られている。iPSはinduced pluripotent stemの頭文字略語（initialism）であるが、IPSではなくiPSなのは、iPodなどのアップル製品のiにあやかってのこと。なお、FIFAやradarのように頭文字をつなげて一単語として発音されるものは頭文字語（acronym）と呼ばれる。それぞれの例を探してみよう。

l.61 Meet the new boss, same as the old boss　The Whoの"Won't get fooled again"（1971年、邦題「無法の世界」）の歌詞の一節。New boss, old bossは何を指すか、また、全体としてどのような意味になるのか考えてみよう。なお、The Whoは1964年結成のイギリスのロックバンドで、特に活動初期には、ライブの最後に楽器を破壊するなどの過激なパフォーマンスで話題となった。ギタリストのピート・タウンゼンドは当時を振り返り、このような破壊活動は見せ掛けのものではなく、新たな時代の音楽を追求した創造的行為だったと述懐している（『ピート・タウンゼンド自伝　フーアイアム』　森田義信訳、2013、河出書房新社）。

l.65 creative destruction　オーストリア生れのアメリカの経済学者 J. A. Schumpeter (1883-1950)の概念。『資本主義・社会主義・民主主義』（1995 中山伊知郎他訳、東洋経済新報社）の第7章を参照。Schumpeterの代表作には、他に『経済発展の理論』（1977 塩野谷祐一他訳、岩波書店）がある。

Unit 7　The Decline of E-Empires

EXERCISES

1　本文に基づいて以下の問いに英語で答えなさい。

1. What was Steve Ballmer's surprise announcement?

2. What did Ballmer say about iPhone in 2007?

3. According to the author, why did Apple charge premium prices for their products?

2　本文に基づいて以下の問いに答えなさい。

1. Windows が選ばれてきた理由は何ですか。また、Microsoftのこれまでの手法について筆者はどう思っていますか。

2. モバイル機器における Apple の商法と OS における Windows の商法に、筆者はどのような類似性を指摘していますか。

3. 筆者はIT業界の覇権の移り変わりにはどのような法則性がありそうだと指摘していますか。

3 CDを聴いて以下の要約文の空欄に適語を入れなさい。

Around 2000, Microsoft was the (　　　　　) company in the computer industry. The reason was something known as network (　　　　　). In other words, people used Windows because so many other people used Windows. If something went wrong, it was easy to find someone to fix the problem. Software and peripheral devices were designed to run on Windows. Apple thought people would buy their products because they were (　　　　　) in quality but more expensive. People, however, bought Windows machines, which were not great but got the job done. This gave Microsoft a (　　　　　) in the industry. But Microsoft failed to grasp the importance of mobile devices, and now Apple has become dominant. In history, we see that strong powers become corrupt and (　　　　　). When that happens, they are replaced by energetic and aggressive newcomers.

4 CDをもう一度聴いてシャドーイングしてみよう。

COLUMN

　本ユニットの著者で経済学者のポール・クルーグマンは、「私の流儀（How I work）」という短いエッセイの中で研究上のポリシーを4つ挙げている。1.「聞く耳を持つ（Listen to the Gentiles）」。すぐれた意見には、壁を作らず柔軟に耳を傾ける。2.「問いを問い直す（Question the question）」。行き詰ったら、課題設定自体を疑う。3.「嘲笑を恐れない（Dare to be silly）」。創造的バカ（creative silliness）を大事にする。4.「極力簡単に（Simplify, simplify）」。できるだけシンプルに考え、平易な言葉で伝える。

　本文中に「創造的破壊（creative destruction）」というJ.A. シュンペーターの有名な概念が使われていたが、流儀の3つ目に挙がっている「創造的バカ」はそのクルーグマン版と言えるもので興味深い。どちらも一見矛盾する語句を並べた撞着語法（oxymoron）と呼ばれる修辞法を用いており、それゆえインパクトの強い表現となっている。

　なお、「私の流儀」はインターネット上で公開されている（http://web.mit.edu/krugman/www/howiwork.html）。

Paul Krugman

UNIT 8 Abu Dhabi Company Searches for Greener Method of Desalination

水がただになる日

By SARA HAMDAN
January 23, 2013

淡水が不足するペルシャ湾岸地域は、飲料水確保に莫大な予算とエネルギーをかけてきた。しかし、近年の技術革新は、より低予算で環境に優しい製法を確立しつつある。その奮闘の様子とともに、地域による水の重みの違いを読み取ろう。

KEYWORDS

2 - 01, 02

A. 記事読解に特に重要な語句の意味を確認しよう。

1. renewable energy
2. the Gulf
3. energy-intensive process
4. seawater desalination
5. filtration technology
6. cost reduction
7. water scarcity
8. the United Arab Emirates
9. sustainable
10. cost-competitive

B. 上下の語群で意味の近いものを結び付け、記事に現れる難易度の高い語句の言い換えを確認しよう。

1. steep ( ) 2. up-front ( ) 3. generate ( )
4. potable ( ) 5. avenue ( ) 6. address (v.) ( )
7. arm ( ) 8. initiative ( ) 9. depleting ( )
10. inexorable ( )

| a. tackle | b. inevitable | c. excessive | d. reducing | e. drinking |
| f. produce | g. way | h. branch | i. program | j. prior |

43

1 ABU DHABI — Masdar, Abu Dhabi's **renewable energy** company, is turning its attention to finding cost-effective ways to remove the salt from seawater, using renewable energy like solar power.

2 There is a huge need for desalination in **the Gulf**, the world's driest region and home to a rapidly growing population. In the desert lands of the Gulf and other parts of the Middle East, drinking water is mostly supplied from **energy-intensive processes** including chemical treatments, thermal distillation and filtration by reverse osmosis. These are all big energy consumers — and can burn up oil, the lifeblood of the region's economy.

3 Because of the steep up-front investments that they have so far required and the high cost per unit of power generated, renewable energy technologies have not been a popular option for producing potable water, in the Gulf or anywhere else. But advances in the technology and a steady decline in manufacturing costs for solar generating plants may be about to change that picture.

4 "While conventional **seawater desalination** methods account for 75 percent of the Gulf's demand for water, the process is energy intensive and costly," Sultan Al Jaber, the chief executive of Masdar, said during an interview. "Coupling renewable energy with the latest in desalination technologies is the logical next step, and it also provides an avenue to spur economic growth and address the region's long-term water security."

5 With financial backing from Abu Dhabi's investment arm Mubadala, Masdar says it plans to build three pilot plants in the next three to four years, sited in different areas of Abu Dhabi, to test innovative technologies and figure out if they have potential for large scale use.

6 Part of the program will focus on a variant of semi-permeable membrane **filtration technology** known as forward osmosis, according to Masdar. Other innovative technologies to be tested will include electrodialysis deionization, membrane distillation and low-temperature distillation, while the program also aims to explore the potential for **cost reductions** and improvements in the energy intensity and efficiency of established technologies such as reverse osmosis.

7 The program aims to bridge the gap between promising technologies which are being developed in universities and research centers, and large-scale industrial applications powered by renewable energy. The long-term goal of the initiative is

to have a facility operating at commercial scale by 2020.

8 Middle Eastern and North African countries are home to 6.3 percent of the world's population, but the region contains only 1.4 percent of the world's fresh water. The Gulf region in particular has the highest **water scarcity** levels in the world, according to the World Bank.

9 With limited surface water and <u>depleting</u> ground water resources, desalination is the key to meeting the <u>inexorable</u> rise in demand for water resulting from economic growth and expanding populations.

10 Already, more than half of all the world's desalination capacity is located in the Arab countries. Yet, in **the United Arab Emirates**, to take just one example, seawater desalination requires about 10 times more energy than pumping water from wells. Costs are projected to increase by 300 percent between 2010 and 2016 according to Masdar's estimates.

11 The energy needed for desalination is usually generated by fossil fuels. The production of drinking water — often to be supplied at subsidized rates — uses 7 percent of global energy, according to the U.S. Department of Energy. So, in effect, large amounts of oil and gas are being used to generate cheap water supplies instead of earning export revenue.

12 "The Middle East is still in the process of addressing its long-term **sustainable** water access and security," Corrado Sommariva, president of the International Desalination Association, said this month at the International Water Summit in Abu Dhabi. "By bridging the gap between research and development and commercialization, Masdar can provide an opportunity for scale-up of technologies that address water access."

13 A handful of other projects in the region also have started to explore the use of renewable energy sources to produce drinking water, but they are costly, few in number and mostly still at the early testing stage.

14 Last June, Eole Water, a French start-up founded in 2008, began field trials in Abu Dhabi of wind turbines designed to produce drinking water from the condensation of atmospheric humidity. The company says a turbine it has developed should be able to pull 1,000 liters of drinking water daily from thin air.

15 The Abu Dhabi trial is intended to test the ability of the technology to stand up to the sandstorms and extreme heat of the harsh desert environment. Other small-scale renewable desalination initiatives in Saudi Arabia and Oman focus either on developing new desalination technologies, or on coupling renewable energy sources with conventional desalination plants. The Masdar project, in contrast, addresses both innovation in water desalination technologies and in renewable energy sources.

16 "For renewable-powered desalination to work, it must be **cost-competitive**," said Mr. Jaber of Masdar. "In our pilot program, we are looking for bankable, commercially viable technologies that can compete in the free market." (822 words)

NOTES

タイトル　Abu Dhabi　UAEを構成する一首長国のアブダビの首都。UAEは、アブダビを始め、ドバイ（Dubai）、ラス・アル・ハイマ（Ras al-Khaimah）など7つの首長国から成る連邦。1971年に各首長国が英国保護領から独立した際にラス・アル・ハイマ以外の6首長国で結成。翌年ラス・アル・ハイマも参加して現在の体制となった。当時、バーレーン（Bahrain）やカタール（Qatar）も連邦参加を協議したが、単独国家としての道を選んだ。UAEにおけるアブダビの特別な地位については、本ユニットのコラムを参照。

l.5 a rapidly growing population　UAE国家統計局（National Bureau of Statistics）の統計によると、2005年に約410万人だったUAEの人口は、僅か3年後の2008年に800万人に達した。注目されるのは増加の内訳で、ほとんど（約380万人）が移住者であった。人口が少ない中で急速な開発を進めるに当たり、UAEは外国人労働者に依存してきた（『アラブ首長国連邦（UAE）を知るための60章』（2011 細井長編著、明石書店）、第30-35章）。

l.21 Mubadala　アブダビの政府系投資開発会社「ムバダラ開発」(Mubadala Developing Company)のこと。2002年設立。公式サイト（http://www.mubadala.com/）によれば、国内外の企業への投資や国内開発の支援を行い、UAEの"diversification"を支援している。

l.36 Middle Eastern and North African countries　食糧農業機関（Food and Agriculture Organization）の2008年のデータを基に小寺正一氏（国立国会図書館調査及び立法考査局：所属は当時）が行った試算では、一人あたりの水資源量は世界平均が $6,500 \, m^3$ に対して、北アフリカ平均は $286 \, m^3$、中東平均が $1,632 \, m^3$ である。この二地域と南アジア（平均 $1,113 \, m^3$）が地域的に最も少ない。スウェーデンの科学者マリン・ファルケンマーク（Malin Falkenmark）によれば、生活に必要な水の量は一人当たり最低 $1,700 \, m^3$ であるが、この三地域はそれを下回っている。なお、最も水資源が豊富な地域は南アメリカで、一人当たり平均 $31,835 \, m^3$ である（小寺正一「水問題をめぐる世界の現状と課題」『レファレンス』No.713、2010年6月号）。

l.39 World Bank　「世界銀行」1994年創設の The International Bank for Reconstruction and Development「国際復興開発銀行」の俗称。

ll.54-55 the International Desalination Association　「国際淡水化協会」公式サイト（https://www.idadesal.org/）によれば、"the world's leading resource for information and professional development for the global desalination industry - and the only global association focused exclusively on desalination and desalination technologies" である。

ll.55-56 the International Water Summit　「国際水サミット」公式サイト（http://iwsabudhabi.com/）によれば、国際水サミットは "a unique global platform for promoting water sustainability in arid regions" である。

Unit 8 Abu Dhabi Company Searches for Greener Method of Desalination

EXERCISES

1 本文に基づいて以下の問いに英語で答えなさい。

1. What is Masdar?

2. How is drinking water mostly supplied in the desert lands of the Gulf and other parts of the Middle East?

3. Why haven't renewable energy technologies been a popular option for producing potable water in these areas?

2 本文に基づいて以下の問いに答えなさい。

1. Masdarはどのような技術を試していますか。

2. Masdarは上記のような新技術により何を目指していますか。

3. Eole Waterはどのような試みをしていますか。

3 CDを聴いて以下の要約文の空欄に適語を入れなさい。　🎧 2-11

Six-point-three percent of the world's population live in the Middle East and North Africa but the region contains only 1.4 percent of the world's fresh water. The (　　　　　) region has the highest water (　　　　　) levels in the world. Desalination is the most important way to meet the rise in demand for water. Desalination requires about 10 times more energy than pumping water from wells. Costs are likely to rise even higher. The energy needed for (　　　　　) is usually generated by fossil fuels, which means that large amounts of oil and gas are used to (　　　　　) cheap water supplies. To solve this problem, some companies are trying to use renewable energy such as solar power. (　　　　　) investment for this technology has been (　　　　　), but technological advances and a decline in manufacturing costs may help.

4 CDをもう一度聴いてシャドーイングしてみよう。　🎧 2-11

COLUMN

　石油産出国としてよく知られるUAEは、2013年現在、世界シェア5.8%（世界第7位）にあたる978億バレルの原油埋蔵量を誇る（BP Statistical Review of Energy 2014の統計）。だが、連邦の7首長国全てが豊富な埋蔵量を持つわけではない。国土面積の差もあり、油田のほとんどはアブダビに集中している。米エネルギー情報局（U.S. Energy Information Administration）によれば、約94%がアブダビで、それに次ぐドバイは僅か4%ほどである。潤沢なオイルマネーでアブダビが連邦全体の経済を支えており、それを反映して同国の首都アブダビが連邦の首都を兼ねる。また、これまで2代の大統領にはいずれもアブダビの首長が選出されている（初代ザーイド・ビン・スルターン・ナヒヤーン、第2代ハリファ・ビン・ザーイド・アール・ナヒヤーン）。

　しかし、UAE最大の都市はと言うと、アブダビではなくドバイ首長国の首都ドバイである。資源が限られるドバイは、早くから物流や観光など石油以外の産業に力を注いできた。パーム・アイランド（人工のリゾート島群）、バージュ・アル・アラブ（最高級ホテル）、ブルジュ・ハリファ（全長828m超の世界最長タワー）などはメディアでよく紹介される。イベント招致も活発で、2020年には中東初の万国博覧会が開かれる。ちなみに、ブルジュ・ハリファは当初ブルジュ・ドバイという名称を予定していたが、アブダビから100億ドルもの資金援助を受けたため、現アブダビ首長の名を冠することとなった。

UNIT 9
British Employers See Value in Europe-Wide Labor Pool
グローバル化の功罪

By STEPHEN CASTLE

June 7, 2013

EU圏内は労働力の移動自由度が高い。本記事では、この政策がイギリスにもたらしているメリット、デメリットが報告されている。少子高齢化が進む日本も徐々に労働力を外国人に頼り始めている。労働力のグローバル化の是非について考えてみよう。

KEYWORDS

2 - 12, 13

A. 記事読解に特に重要な語句の意味を確認しよう。

1. multinational company
2. European Union
3. recruitment
4. labor pool
5. immigration
6. ex-Communist country
7. European Commission
8. single market
9. Pan-European
10. hiring

B. 上下の語群で意味の近いものを結び付け、記事に現れる難易度の高い語句の言い換えを確認しよう。

1. lapse ( )
2. revenue ( )
3. contentious ( )
4. influx ( )
5. menial ( )
6. meddlesome ( )
7. abide by ( )
8. outweigh ( )
9. vexation ( )
10. zilch ( )

a. zero	b. surpass	c. expire
d. obey		
e. controversial	f. cause of annoyance	g. flow
h. interfering		
i. income	j. low-skilled	

49

[1] LONDON — With several big construction projects under way in Britain, the **multinational company** CH2M Hill spent six months searching for a qualified tunneling engineer.

[2] Only a few weeks ago did the company find a candidate, in Portugal. CH2M Hill quickly made plans to bring him north — no visa or work permits were required, thanks to a **European Union** policy that allows the free flow of labor across the borders of the 27-country bloc.

[3] With signs that Britain might seek an exit from the European Union, businesses like CH2M Hill are starting to focus on what they might lose in the labor force if the country does leave.

[4] For non-Europeans, securing a work permit can take three months, so the labor law is a huge help, said Michael I. Glenn, CH2M Hill's director of international operations. "These programs and projects that we do are of a scale that we have to move our expertise around," he said.

[5] Continental Europe provides a nearby pool of potential employees with the qualifications needed to work in Britain, added Andrea Laws, the company's director of international **recruitment**.

Andrea Laws

[6] Britain, with 61.9 million people, has about 40.6 million people of working age. But together, the 27 countries in the European Union, population 494.9 million, represent a **labor pool** of about 329.7 million. (Only citizens of Romania and Bulgaria are restricted from working freely in Britain, and they will gain that right in January when temporary restrictions imposed by Britain lapse.)

[7] Despite Britain's unemployment rate of 7.8 percent, many businesses say that without access to the European Union's labor pool, filling all sorts of jobs would be difficult, either because they cannot find enough people with the right skills in Britain or because there are some jobs that Britons are reluctant to do.

[8] A report this month from the London Chamber of Commerce and Industry concluded that Britain's leaving the European Union would directly affect "firms' ability to do business," "their access to skills" and, therefore, the British government's tax revenue.

[9] The report also said the 2.2 million European Union immigrants were "much

more likely" to be employed and less likely to be reliant on public welfare benefits than either British citizens or immigrants from outside the European Union.

10 But as in the United States, where **immigration** legislation has been hotly debated for months, migrant labor remains a contentious issue in Britain. A growing populist force, the U.K. Independence Party, blames Europe for allowing hundreds of thousands of workers outside the country to settle here.

11 "The business perspective, broadly speaking, clashes with the No. 1 concern about the European Union from the public," said Mats Persson, director of Open Europe, which favors a looser relationship between Britain and the European Union.

12 British opponents of open borders point to the large influx of workers from the former Communist states of Eastern Europe in the last decade. When Poland and seven other **ex-Communist countries** joined the European Union in 2004, the British government underestimated the scale of migration and chose not to impose temporary work restrictions.

13 Yet in the chamber report, a director of a promotional merchandise company said "a number of our suppliers use Polish or Baltic workers to do quite menial tasks because they cannot get local people to do them."

14 Big British employers of foreign labor include service businesses like hotels because, the report said, part of the problem with such sectors "is their poor image and the belief that they do not offer career progression opportunities."

15 Still, many British business leaders criticize what they consider meddlesome employment rules by the European Union, like rules on maximum working hours and workplace rights for staff members on temporary contracts.

16 But the **European Commission** takes a different view. To expect access to the European Union's **single market** without abiding by its social and employment legislation is "not realistic," said Jonathan Todd, a commission spokesman. For many employers, the advantages of a **Pan-European** work force outweigh bureaucratic vexations.

17 Consider Z-Card, which sells information and advertising materials mostly in the form of pocket-size foldout cards. The company is privately held, with annual revenue of about £6 million, or $9.3 million, and has a staff of 34. Only 16 are Britons. The rest are mainly from other countries in the European Union.

18 While Britain is the company's biggest individual market, 70 percent of

its business comes from other European Union countries, with clients like the German airline Lufthansa and the Vatican. (Z-Card produced a foldout brochure of tourist information for the Vatican Library.)

19 The likelihood that a Briton could have secured the Vatican contract, the company's managing director, Liz Love, said would have been "absolutely <u>zilch</u>." For CH2M Hill, which has 28,000 employees and made $7 billion in revenue last year, the **hiring** challenge is less a question of culture than of capabilities. Needing to recruit at least 500 people in Britain this year for construction jobs it has already won, the company is constrained by a shortage of engineers, partly because engineering has not been a popular field of study in the country's universities.

20 Ms. Laws said the company was in a global "war for talent." Construction booms in the Middle East, Asia and Latin America are pulling experienced engineers away from Europe, she said.

21 Mr. Glenn said the European Union not only enabled CH2M Hill to hire for Britain from the Continent but also let the company easily move employees to other European countries once projects were finished. That helps it retain skilled engineers. "The skills base we are talking about and the scale of the programs require us to be able to move folks around," he said. "The visa issue is significant." (943 words)

NOTES

l.10 labor force　work force/workforce と同義。force は「力」が中心義であるが、そこからこの例のように「力を持つ集団、組織」へと意味が広がる。同様の force の用法は academic force、air force、Self Defence Force、police force、sales force など多くの表現に見られる。なお、labor force は Unit 3 で既出。

l.30 the London Chamber of Commerce and Industry「ロンドン商工会議所」1881 年設立。語学、情報学、金融等に関する様々な国際的資格試験を実施していることで知られる。

l.37 But as in the United States　長らく不法移民に悩むアメリカの上院で、移民制度改革法案が 2013 年 6 月に可決された。その内容は、現在滞在している不法移民に合法的立場（市民権）獲得の道を開くとともに、国境警備の強化などにより今後の不法移住を規制するというものである。本法案を起草した Charles E. Shumer, John McCain ら超党派 8 人の上院議員は "Gang of Eight" と呼ばれる。

l.39 the U.K. Independence Party「英国独立党」反 EU を掲げる英国の政党（略称 UKIP）。1993 年結党。現党首はナイジェル・ファラージ（Nigel Farage）。UKIP については、本ユニットのコラムも参照。

ll.42–43 Open Europe「オープンヨーロッパ」2005 年設立のシンクタンク。本部をロンドンとブリュッセルに置く。EU の政治、経済について研究している。公式サイト（http://www.openeurope.org.uk/）には以下のような説明がある。"Open Europe is an independent think tank, with offices in London and Brussels, set up by leading UK business people to contribute positive new thinking to the debate about the future direction of the European Union."

Unit 9 British Employers See Value in Europe-Wide Labor Pool

EXERCISES

1 本文に基づいて以下の問いに英語で答えなさい。

1. Why was CH2M Hill quickly able to make plans to bring the Portuguese candidate to Britain?

2. Why do many businesses say that without access to the European Union's labor pool, filling all sorts of jobs would be difficult in Britain?

3. Why was there a large influx of workers from the former Communist states of Eastern Europe into England in the last decade?

2 本文に基づいて以下の問いに答えなさい。

1. EU圏内の労働（雇用）にはどのような取り決めがありますか。

2. 1の取り決めに対し、どのような賛成・反対意見がありますか。

3. CH2M HillはEUの雇用の取り決めにより、どのような恩恵を受けていますか。

3 CDを聴いて以下の要約文の空欄に適語を入れなさい。

Some British companies are worried that Britain might seek an exit from the European (　　　　　). Continental Europe provides a pool of potential workers with the qualifications needed to work in Britain. Despite Britain's (　　　　　) rate of 7.8 percent, many businesses would find it hard to fill job vacancies because they cannot find enough British people with the right skills or because there are some jobs that Britons are (　　　　　) to do. British people who oppose open borders point to the large (　　　　　) of workers from Eastern Europe. But a number of companies use such workers to do (　　　　　) tasks because local people will not do them. British employers of foreign labor include service businesses like hotels because such sectors have a poor image and people believe they do not offer opportunities for career (　　　　　).

4 CDをもう一度聴いてシャドーイングしてみよう。

COLUMN

　欧州共同体（EU）は拡大を続けている。1993年のマーストリヒト条約発効時に12カ国だった加盟数は、2014年現在、二倍超の28カ国である。2004年には中東欧8カ国を含む10カ国が一気に加盟した。これは1989年の冷戦終結により実現した歴史的な東西融合であった。こうした長年に渡る「国家間の友愛関係（fraternity between nations）」構築を進めた功績により、EUは2012年にノーベル平和賞を受賞した。地域共同体としては初の平和賞受賞であった。
　拡大は様々な成果を上げている一方で課題も多い。例えば、本文にあったように、移民の急増（に対する危惧）が社会不安を引き起こしている。これが一つの理由となり、昨今EU懐疑派が注目を集めている。イギリスでは、英国独立党（U.K. Independence Party）が支持を高め、2014年に行われた欧州議会選挙では保守党と労働党という二大政党を抑えイギリス第一党となった。同選挙では、他国でも、フランスの国民戦線（Front National）やデンマークの国民党（Dansk Folkeparti）などのEUに懐疑的な政党が躍進した。
　EUの拡大は今後も続く。2014年現在、アイスランド、アルバニア、セルビア、トルコ、マケドニア旧ユーゴスラビア共和国、モンテネグロの6カ国が加盟候補国（candidate countries）として加盟に向けて交渉中である。この内最も苦労しているのはトルコであろう。1987年に加盟申請し、6カ国中最も早く1999年から加盟候補国であるが、キプロス問題などでなかなか交渉が進まず現在に至っている。

UNIT 10

Hopes for Renewal in Japan, but Also a Host of Challenges

オリンピックは来たけれど

By HIROKO TABUCHI and JOSHUA HUNT   September 7, 2013

2020年に夏季五輪が東京で開催される。56年ぶり2度目だ。開催決定に対する見方は海外と国内では異なる。国内でも立場により様々。立場により異なる多様な捉え方を読み取り、五輪招致について改めて考えよう。

KEYWORDS

2 - 24, 25

A. 記事読解に特に重要な語句の意味を確認しよう。

1. host the 2020 Summer Games
2. government debt
3. the rejuvenation of Japan
4. contamination
5. the Fukushima nuclear disaster
6. deficit spending
7. compact Olympics
8. economic recovery
9. Fukushima refugee
10. play down

B. 上下の語群で意味の近いものを結び付け、記事に現れる難易度の高い語句の言い換えを確認しよう。

1. erupt ( )   2. scrutiny ( )   3. containment ( )
4. stricken ( )   5. revelation ( )   6. pall ( )
7. haunting ( )   8. allay ( )   9. opportune ( )
10. bolster ( )

a. examination	b. support	c. control	d. crippled
e. calm	f. burst	g. exposure	h. timely
i. memorable	j. shadow		

55

[1] TOKYO — The sun rose at 5:18 a.m. Sunday in the Japanese capital. A minute later came the good news.

[2] For the second time, Tokyo is set to be the home of the Summer Olympics, after members of the International Olympic Committee overwhelmingly picked the city above Istanbul and Madrid to **host the 2020 Summer Games**.

[3] As alerts went out to smartphones across the still-drowsy city, about 2,000 locals at a gymnasium who had awaited the I.O.C. decision overnight erupted in cheers. "We're very happy to host the Olympics in 2020," said Kosei Tomiyama, a Tokyo retiree. "I'm 79 years old, and this really gives me something to look forward to. I really hope I live long enough to see it. Tokyo has everything you need, plus it's safe."

[4] The awarding of the Games to Tokyo, the sprawling Japanese metropolis of 13 million people, is a welcome boost for the nation after the tsunami and nuclear disaster that laid waste to its northern Pacific coast two years ago.

[5] But the Olympics will heighten global scrutiny of Japan's containment and cleanup efforts at the stricken Fukushima Daiichi Nuclear Power Plant, about 155 miles north of Tokyo. Recent revelations of leaks of contaminated water from the site had cast a pall on Tokyo's bid in its final weeks.

[6] The 2020 Games will also increase pressure on Japan to put its public finances in order. Japan's **government debt** has increased to more than twice the size of its $6 trillion economy, in large part because of the costs of caring for the country's increasingly elderly population. Tokyo's organizing committee has budgeted the Olympics at about $10 billion, including the cost of constructing venues and improving transport infrastructure.

[7] "The 2020 Olympics will represent **the rejuvenation of Japan** after the haunting disaster," said Ken Ruoff, director of the Center for Japanese Studies at Portland State University.

[8] He added, "The main challenge, in addition to allaying fears about **contamination** from **the Fukushima nuclear disaster**, may be justifying the expense at a time when Japan has already set new records for **deficit spending**."

[9] Still, the Olympics could not come to the Japanese capital at a more opportune time. Tokyo last hosted the Summer Games in 1964, signaling its transformation into a modern city after the destruction of World War II. In the half-century

since, Japan developed into a global economic powerhouse, only to see growth stall in what has come to be called Japan's two lost decades.

[10] But since Prime Minister Shinzo Abe came to power late last year and unleashed bold monetary and government reforms to jump-start the economy, Japan has gone from a global economic laggard to the fastest-growing country in the Group of 7. Winning the 2020 Games is expected to further bolster the standing of the popular Abe, who flew to Buenos Aires to lead Tokyo's final pitch to the I.O.C.

[11] Economists at Nomura, the Japanese investment bank, said they expected the 2020 Olympics to add about $14 billion to Japan's economy — a lower percentage of gross domestic product than the boost the country got from its previous three Olympic Games: the Summer Games in Tokyo in 1964, and the Winter Games in Sapporo in 1972 and in Nagano in 1998.

[12] Tokyo's bid centered on the vision of a "**compact Olympics**" that will reuse some of the venues that remain from 1964 to cut back on new investment, but also limiting the event's economic impact.

[13] Still, hosting the Olympic Games could bring a wide range of other benefits, including restoring Tokyo's social standing, which could eventually feed into the Japanese economy, Hiromichi Tamura and his colleagues at Nomura said in a research note. News of the Games will also go a long way to brightening the mood here and fueling more consumer confidence and spending, a missing part of the puzzle in Japan's **economic recovery** so far, they said.

[14] "If the government's growth strategies go according to plan, the benefits should be obvious to everyone" by 2020, they said. "In the same way that the 1964 Tokyo Olympics showed that Japan had entered the ranks of modern industrialized nations, the 2020 Tokyo Olympics could show that Japan is back."

[15] Not everybody is celebrating. "They continue to ignore the severe problems at Fukushima," said Kazuko Nihei, 37, a housewife and **Fukushima refugee** who lives in Tokyo and was quoted on the local Tokyo Shimbun Web site. "They are taking us for fools."

[16] Earlier, in Buenos Aires, where the Olympic vote was announced, Abe appeared to **play down** the issue. He said the government had a comprehensive cleanup plan in place. "The bottom line is that there is absolutely no problem,"

he said. "Please look at the facts, not newspaper headlines."

70 **17** The Japanese news media seemed to have smaller concerns. "English is going to be necessary around town," a young newscaster gushed on the Tokyo Broadcasting System. "Let's start learning English. You may be asked for directions on the streets." (824 words)

NOTES

l.12 sprawling　スプロール化は都市が無計画で無秩序に広がることを表す都市工学用語。「手足を無造作に伸ばして座ったり、横になる」という原義からのメタファー。スプロール化現象は、東京に限らず国内外の大都市一般でよく起きる現象である。

l.35 economic powerhouse　powerhouseは掛詞のように読める。原義を基に考えてみよう。

l.36 Japan's two lost decades　いわゆる「バブル崩壊」による1990年代の不況期が「失われた10年」と呼ばれたが、その後2000年代に入っても景気が回復しなかったため、この20年は「失われた20年」と呼ばれる。

l.38 jump-start the economy　jump-startは、本来は「バッテリー切れなどで動かなくなった自動車をブースターケーブル（jump(er) leads）を使って動かす」ことを表す。それを踏まえ、日本経済がどのように捉えられているかを考えてみよう。

l.40 Group of 7　日本、イギリス、アメリカ、ドイツ、フランス、イタリア、カナダにより構成される。通称G7。本来はこの7カ国の財務相、中央銀行総裁会議を指すが、ここでは単に当該7カ国を指す。なお、この会議は、当初は、日本、イギリス、アメリカ、ドイツ、フランス（G5）で始まり、1986年からイタリアとカナダが加わった。

l.48 the vision of a "compact Olympics"　本文では財政面の記述のみだが、第一義的には、物理的に「コンパクト」であること、つまり、選手と観客の移動距離を少なくするために、競技施設等を集中させることを指す。東京の『立候補ファイル』（第1巻2.2節）には、「東京圏にある33競技会場のうち28会場、全てのIOCホテル及びIPCホテルが選手村から半径8km圏内に存在する」という「大都市の中心でかつてないほどコンパクトな大会」とある。しかし、その後、建設費や人件費が高騰したことなどにより、舛添要一東京都知事は2014年6月にこのスローガンにとらわれない会場整備計画の見直しを表明した。

l.63 housewife　女性は家庭にいるものという連想に結びつくため、使用が避けられる場合がある。その場合には、homemaker, householder, home manager などを用いる。Unit 4 (l. 94)の注も参照。この事例のように、欧米が、男性や白人、西欧中心の考え方をしてきたことを反省して、女性や、アジア系・アフリカ系民族、同性愛者などを尊重し、それを反映した言動をしようとすることを政治的公正（Political Correctness, PC）という。他のどのような表現に見られるか考えてみよう。

l.70 smaller concerns　この箇所の比較級（smaller）は何との比較か考えよう。また、これ以降の内容には筆者のどのような気持ち、見方が込められているか考えてみよう。

Unit 10 Hopes for Renewal in Japan, but Also a Host of Challenges

EXERCISES

1 本文に基づいて以下の問いに英語で答えなさい。

1. Who is Kosei Tomiyama?

2. What did Tomiyama say about the awarding of the Games to Tokyo?

3. So far, Japan has hosted three Olympic Games. When and Where?

2 本文に基づいて以下の問いに答えなさい。

1. 東京での五輪開催にはどのような課題がありますか。

2. 東京での五輪開催にはどのような経済効果があると考えられますか。

3. なぜ Nihei Kazuko さんは、五輪の東京開催の決定を喜んでいないのですか。

3 CDを聴いて以下の要約文の空欄に適語を入れなさい。

The awarding of the Games to Tokyo is a welcome boost for the country after the tsunami and nuclear (　　　　　) in 2011. After Tokyo last hosted the Games in 1964, the country was transformed into a modern city after the effects of World War II. After that, growth stalled and Japan suffered two lost (　　　　　). Economists said they expected the 2020 Olympics to add about $14 billion to Japan's economy. Tokyo has a vision of a "compact Olympics" reusing (　　　　　) from 1964 to cut back on new investment. Hosting the Olympics could bring other benefits, including brightening the mood here and fueling consumer (　　　　　) and spending. But not everybody is celebrating. Some people believe the government is continuing to ignore problems at Fukushima. But Prime Minister Abe said the government had a (　　　　　) plan.

4 CDをもう一度聴いてシャドーイングしてみよう。

COLUMN

　2020年の東京オリンピックは夏季大会としては1964年以来2度目の開催となるが、招致決定はこれが3度目である。1940年の第12回大会も東京は招致に成功した。しかし、このときは盧溝橋事件などにより国内外から反対の声が上がり開催権を返上した。その後、東京と招致を争ったヘルシンキが代替開催地となったが、結局、第二次世界大戦が勃発し中止された。

　1940年には第5回冬季オリンピックも日本（札幌）で開催される予定だった。このときはまだ冬季大会と夏季大会が同一年開催であり、当時のオリンピック憲章により、夏季大会の開催地に冬季大会の優先的開催権が与えられていたからである。だが、これも夏季大会と同じく返上となった。1940年は日本書紀に記される神武天皇即位の年から2600年目（皇紀2600年）に当たり、オリンピック招致はその国家的記念行事として企図された。その後オリンピックを開催するまでに東京は24年、札幌は32年を要した。

　当時の経過については、『幻の東京オリンピック』（橋本一夫、1994、NHKブックス）、アジア歴史資料センター公式サイト（http://www.jacar.go.jp/）の特集「東京オリンピック、1940年〜幻のオリンピックへ〜」、「1940年幻の札幌オリンピック招致運動について」（新井博、2014、『びわこ成蹊スポーツ大学研究紀要』第11号）が詳しい。

UNIT 11

Madrid and Istanbul Respond Differently to Rejection by Olympics

オリンピックを招致するということ

By RAPHAEL MINDER and CEYLAN YEGINSU

September 8, 2013

東京と五輪開催を争ったマドリードとイスタンブール。両都市の招致失敗の受け止め方は大きく異なる。また、招致に対する考え方も大きく異なる。招致できれば成功、招致できなければ失敗、という図式は必ずしもスペインとトルコの二国にはない。その違いを捉えよう。

KEYWORDS

2 - 35, 36

A. 記事読解に特に重要な語句の意味を確認しよう。

1. unemployment
2. recession
3. environmental concern
4. Olympic venue
5. debt
6. budget overrun
7. doping
8. Olympic bid
9. ecological consideration
10. deforestation

B. 上下の語群で意味の近いものを結び付け、記事に現れる難易度の高い語句の言い換えを確認しよう。

1. scramble ( )
2. underused ( )
3. halt ( )
4. ballot ( )
5. comply with ( )
6. disenchantment ( )
7. raze ( )
8. devoid of ( )
9. legacy ( )
10. assessment ( )

a. lacking	b. try	c. destroy	d. evaluation
e. obey	f. stop	g. inheritance	h. disappointment
i. underexploited	j. vote		

[1] MADRID — Madrid and Istanbul started counting the costs on Sunday of failing once more to be named an Olympic host, after Tokyo was chosen to organize the 2020 Games.

[2] That cost could be higher for Madrid, whose population, hit hard by record **unemployment** and a long **recession**, had rallied around the idea that the Games could help create jobs and revive the image and economy of Spain.

[3] In contrast, large groups of people in the central Taksim district in Istanbul celebrated their city's Olympic defeat on Saturday night. They argued that the Turkish government had tried to use the Olympics as an excuse to ignore **environmental concerns** and proceed with large-scale building projects.

[4] With 80 percent of its earmarked **Olympic venues** already completed, Madrid's bid was centered on a straightforward argument: we have built the sites already, so let us at least use them.

[5] Madrid, Spain's capital and largest city, now faces a new challenge, as it scrambles to reduce $9.2 billion in **debt** as it figures out what to do with some of its half-built or underused sports centers, including a water sports complex that was to serve as the Olympic swimming pool. Construction on the aquatic center started in 2004, but the work was halted four years later amid **budget overruns** as Spain's construction bubble burst.

[6] Among Madrid's other underexploited flagship sites is the Caja Mágica, or Magic Box, a tennis center with a retractable roof that opened in 2009, with intentions of holding Olympic events. The center ended up costing $387 million, compared with an initial budget of $158 million, but it has been used little since, except for a Masters tennis tournament held each May.

[7] The voting was carried out in Buenos Aires by secret ballot, making it impossible to know why members of the International Olympic Committee favored Tokyo over Istanbul and Madrid. But a negative factor shared by the two losing cities, their countries' response to **doping** in sports, might have played a role.

[8] Turkey recently announced a "zero tolerance" stance on doping after a string of positive test results that led to the ban of more than 30 athletes by the Turkish Athletics Federation. In 2011, however, Turkey lost its World Anti-Doping Agency accreditation after failing to comply with international standards.

[9] A Spanish judge fueled international criticism in April, when she ordered

that about 200 bags of blood and plasma be destroyed instead of handing them over to antidoping inspectors. The bags were among evidence seized by the police during a cycling investigation focusing on Eufemiano Fuentes, a Spanish doctor found guilty of endangering public health by providing blood transfusions to cyclists. During his trial, Fuentes said his list of clients also included unnamed athletes from soccer, tennis, boxing and track and field.

10 The Madrid delegation hoped that the investigation had been put to rest, but the doping issue was raised Saturday before the vote in Buenos Aires, both during Madrid's presentation to the Olympic delegates and in a news conference.

11 A few hours later, after Madrid was rejected, <u>disenchantment</u> and sadness spread rapidly among the large crowd that had gathered around Puerta de Alcalá, one of Madrid's landmarks, where local musicians performed before the vote.

12 In Istanbul, however, recent social divisions were highlighted Saturday as supporters and opponents of the Olympics gathered at separate sites. After Istanbul failed in its fifth **Olympic bid**, some cried and others embraced in the ancient square of Sultanahmet. Most just stood still, lowering their Turkish flags.

13 In Taksim Square, those who had opposed the bid celebrated late into the night. Taksim had been turned into a battleground in June after disputes over the <u>razing</u> of a public park evolved into the largest antigovernment rally the country had had in more than a decade. Analysts have said that one of the largest setbacks for Turkey's Olympic bid was the government's harsh crackdown on the protesters.

14 "We've been tear-gassed too many times to have any Olympic spirit left in us," said Ali Turan, an architect who has been active with the "Boycott Istanbul 2020" campaign in Istanbul. "This city has to learn to value its people and environment before it makes any promises to the world."

15 The campaign was led by a group of urban planners and architects who carried out an assessment of Istanbul's candidate file and concluded that it was a "megaconstruction pitch," <u>devoid of</u> the Olympic ideals of <u>legacy</u>, spirit and sustainability.

16 "In Turkey's candidate file, there are no environmental <u>assessments</u>, no **ecological consideration** or evaluations of social impacts for those that will

be displaced from their homes," the group said via e-mail.

70 **17** Separately, clashes between the police and students at Middle East Technical University in Ankara began Friday and continued into Saturday, with the police firing tear gas and water cannons at demonstrators who were protesting **deforestation** on their campus. The deforestation was led by the city to accommodate a road project. After the Olympic vote, Ankara's mayor, Melih
75 Gokcek, wrote on Twitter that the antigovernment protesters were traitors who caused Istanbul to lose its bid. (842 words)

NOTES

l.32 World Anti-Doping Agency　「世界反ドーピング機関」通称WADA。1998年のツール・ド・フランス（Tour de France）での薬物スキャンダルがきっかけで、1999年に創設された。本部はカナダのモントリオール。公式サイト（https://www.wada-ama.org/）には禁止薬物・手法の一覧（Prohibited List）が掲載されている。

l.37 Eufemiano Fuentes　「ウフェミアーノ・フエンテス」2006年にスペイン警察が大規模なドーピング捜査を行い、自転車競技を始めとする数多くのスポーツ選手のドーピング関与とそれを組織していた医師（Fuentes）の存在が明らかになった。その結果、Fuentesは2010年に公衆衛生違反の容疑で逮捕、起訴された。摘発当時のスペインにはドーピングを禁止する法律がなかったため、容疑は公衆衛生違反に留まった（事件の半年後にドーピングを禁じる法律ができた）。関与した多くの選手が行っていたのが自己血輸血であった。その証拠として押収された保存血液バッグに関し、裁判所は告発容疑の関係で違反選手の特定などに使うことはできないと判断。文中にあるように廃棄を命じた。この事件に関しては、『トップ・アスリートの赤い闇　血液ドーピングなしには勝てない』（2013 酒瀬川亮介、由利英明、朝日新聞デジタル**SELECT**）、『シークレット・レース』（2013　タイラー・ハミルトン、ダニエル・コイル著、児島修訳、小学館文庫）が詳しい。『シークレット・レース』の著者の一人であるタイラー・ハミルトンは、アテネ五輪自転車競技金メダリスト（後にドーピング問題で取り消しとなった）。昨今のドーピングについては、本ユニットのコラムを参照。

l.59 Olympic spirit　例えば、オリンピック憲章（Olympic Charter）のオリンピズムの根本原則（fundamental principles of Olympism）の項目1、2には以下のように述べられている。"1. Olympism is a philosophy of life, exalting and combining in a balanced whole the qualities of body, will and mind. Blending sport with culture and education, Olympism seeks to create a way of life based on the joy of effort, the educational value of good example, social responsibility and respect for universal fundamental ethical principles. 2. The goal of Olympism is to place sport at the service of the harmonious development of humankind, with a view to promoting a peaceful society concerned with the preservation of human dignity." オリンピック憲章は、オリンピックムーブメント公式サイト（http://www.olympic.org/）から入手可能。

l.64 candidate file　「立候補ファイル」立候補に当たりIOCに提出する概要説明文書一式。東京オリンピック・パラリンピック競技大会招致委員会が今回の立候補に当たり提出したものは、同委員会の公式サイト（http://tokyo2020.jp/jp/）から入手可能。

Unit 11　Madrid and Istanbul Respond Differently to Rejection by Olympics

EXERCISES

1　本文に基づいて以下の問いに英語で答えなさい。

1. What did people in Madrid expect the 2020 Games to do?

2. Why did large groups of people in the central Taksim district in Istanbul celebrate their city's Olympic defeat?

3. What did Ankara's mayor, Melih Gokcek, write on Twitter after the Olympic vote?

2　本文に基づいて以下の問いに答えなさい。

1. マドリードとイスタンブールに共通する落選要因と考えられるのは何ですか。また、それに関してどのようなことがそれぞれの国でありましたか。

2. イスタンブールには、さらにどのような落選要因があったと考えられますか。また、それに関して具体的にどのような出来事がありましたか。

3. Boycott Istanbul 2020 とはどのような運動ですか。また、その関係者はイスタンブールの招致をどのように捉えていますか。

3 CDを聴いて以下の要約文の空欄に適語を入れなさい。　　　　2-44

Madrid and Istanbul failed to become (　　　　　　　) of the 2020 Games. The people of Madrid thought the Games could help create jobs and revive Spain. In Istanbul large crowds celebrated because they thought the Turkish government had tried to use the Olympics as an excuse to ignore (　　　　　　　) concerns. A negative factor shared by the two cities is their countries' response to use of drugs in sports. In 2011 Turkey failed to (　　　　　　　) with international antidoping standards. In Spain, a judge refused to hand over blood samples to antidoping inspectors. Also, in Istanbul in June, disputes over the razing of a public park turned into a big (　　　　　　　) rally. Analysts said that the government's harsh crackdown on the protesters was a large setback for Turkey's Olympic (　　　　　　　).

4 CDをもう一度聴いてシャドーイングしてみよう。　　　　2-44

COLUMN

　従来のドーピングは、筋肉増強剤や興奮剤などの禁止薬物（dope）の投与だった。しかし、近年はそうした薬物の使用に留まらない。中でも蔓延しているのは、血液を増加させ、持久力を向上させるエリスロポエチン（erythropoietin、EPO）の投与である。最近ではEPOの代わりに血液自体も使われる。つまり、いったん自分の血液を抜いて保存し、血液量回復後に戻すことで赤血球を増加させる。いわゆる「血液ドーピング」である。今やこうした物質レベルを超え、遺伝子ドーピングまでもあると言う。

　ドーピングの手段として取り上げられることが増えたEPOであるが、本来は腎性貧血の治療薬である。現在も世界中の透析患者の命を支える。その開発に多大な貢献をしたのは、日本人医学者の宮家隆次氏（元熊本大学講師、カリフォルニア大学サンタバーバラ校教授）。氏が中心となり再生不良性貧血患者の尿2.5トンから抽出された約10mgのEPOが研究を飛躍的に進展させ、医薬品としての普及に結実した。宮家氏のEPO精製までの苦労については川北誠氏（熊本第一病院理事長）の「エリスロポエチン物語―純化の歩みと遺伝子クローニングへの道のり―」（第75回日本血液学会における基調講演：オンラインで閲覧可能）が詳しい。

UNIT 12

Need a Job? Invent It

「仕事を創る」という発想

By THOMAS L. FRIEDMAN　　　　March 30, 2013

グローバル化が進み、人材は世界中から集まる。一方、知識はネット上で拾うものになってきた。そういう社会では、仕事は「就く」ものではなく、「創る」ものという発想が重要だと言う。それはどういうことか？そうした社会で求められる能力とその開発を可能にする教育とはどのようなものか？

KEYWORDS

2 - 45, 46

A. 記事読解に特に重要な語句の意味を確認しよう。

1. K-12
2. high-skilled job
3. innovation ready
4. critical thinking
5. collaboration
6. reimagine
7. education reform
8. intrinsic motivation
9. entrepreneurship
10. innovative economy

B. 上下の語群で意味の近いものを結び付け、記事に現れる難易度の高い語句の言い換えを確認しよう。

1. matter (v.)　( )　2. sustain　( )　3. obsolete　( )
4. tall　( )　5. elaborate (v.)　( )　6. persistent　( )
7. disposition　( )　8. ingredients　( )　9. affiliate　( )
10. consortium　( )

a. out of date　b. association　c. material　d. keep
e. give more details　f. attach　g. temperament　h. be important
i. extravagant
j. persevering

1 WHEN Tony Wagner, the Harvard education specialist, describes his job today, he says he's "a translator between two hostile tribes" — the education world and the business world, the people who teach our kids and the people who give them jobs. Wagner's argument in his book "Creating Innovators: The Making of Young People Who Will Change the World" is that our **K-12** and college tracks are not consistently "adding the value and teaching the skills that matter most in the marketplace."

2 This is dangerous at a time when there is increasingly no such thing as a high-wage, middle-skilled job — the thing that sustained the middle class in the last generation. Now there is only a high-wage, **high-skilled job**. Every middle-class job today is being pulled up, out or down faster than ever. That is, it either requires more skill or can be done by more people around the world or is being buried — made obsolete — faster than ever. Which is why the goal of education today, argues Wagner, should not be to make every child "college ready" but **"innovation ready"** — ready to add value to whatever they do.

3 That is a tall task. I tracked Wagner down and asked him to elaborate. "Today," he said via e-mail, "because knowledge is available on every Internet-connected device, what you know matters far less than what you can do with what you know. The capacity to innovate — the ability to solve problems creatively or bring new possibilities to life — and skills like **critical thinking**, communication and **collaboration** are far more important than academic knowledge. As one executive told me, 'We can teach new hires the content, and we will have to because it continues to change, but we can't teach them how to think — to ask the right questions — and to take initiative.'"

4 My generation had it easy. We got to "find" a job. But, more than ever, our kids will have to "invent" a job. (Fortunately, in today's world, that's easier and cheaper than ever before.) Sure, the lucky ones will find their first job, but, given the pace of change today, even they will have to reinvent, re-engineer and **reimagine** that job much more often than their parents if they want to advance in it. If that's true, I asked Wagner, what do young people need to know today?

5 "Every young person will continue to need basic knowledge, of course," he said. "But they will need skills and motivation even more. Of these three education goals, motivation is the most critical. Young people who are intrinsically motivated — curious, persistent, and willing to take risks — will learn new knowledge and skills continuously. They will be able to find new opportunities or create their own — a <u>disposition</u> that will be increasingly important as many traditional careers disappear."

[6] So what should be the focus of **education reform** today?

[7] "We teach and test things most students have no interest in and will never need, and facts that they can Google and will forget as soon as the test is over," said Wagner. "Because of this, the longer kids are in school, the less motivated they become. Gallup's recent survey showed student engagement going from 80 percent in fifth grade to 40 percent in high school. More than a century ago, we 'reinvented' the one-room schoolhouse and created factory schools for the industrial economy. Reimagining schools for the 21st-century must be our highest priority. We need to focus more on teaching the skill and will to learn and to make a difference and bring the three most powerful <u>ingredients</u> of **intrinsic motivation** into the classroom: play, passion and purpose."

[8] What does that mean for teachers and principals?

[9] "Teachers," he said, "need to coach students to performance excellence, and principals must be instructional leaders who create the culture of collaboration required to innovate. But what gets tested is what gets taught, and so we need 'Accountability 2.0.' All students should have digital portfolios to show evidence of mastery of skills like critical thinking and communication, which they build up right through K-12 and postsecondary. Selective use of high-quality tests, like the College and Work Readiness Assessment, is important. Finally, teachers should be judged on evidence of improvement in students' work through the year — instead of a score on a bubble test in May. We need lab schools where students earn a high school diploma by completing a series of skill-based 'merit badges' in things like **entrepreneurship**. And schools of education where all new teachers have 'residencies' with master teachers and performance standards — not content standards — must become the new normal throughout the system."

[10] Who is doing it right?

[11] "Finland is one of the most **innovative economies** in the world," he said, "and it is the only country where students leave high school 'innovation-ready.' They learn concepts and creativity more than facts, and have a choice of many electives — all with a shorter school day, little homework, and almost no testing. In the U.S., 500 K-12 schools <u>affiliated</u> with Hewlett Foundation's Deeper

Learning Initiative and a consortium of 100 school districts called EdLeader21 are developing new approaches to teaching 21st-century skills. There are also a growing number of 'reinvented' colleges like the Olin College of Engineering, the M.I.T. Media Lab and the 'D-school' at Stanford where students learn to innovate." (882 words)

NOTES

Thomas L. Friedman　「トマス・L・フリードマン」アメリカのコラムニスト、ジャーナリスト、作家。オックスフォード大学修了後、UPI記者、New York Times記者を経て、1995年より同社外交問題コラム（Foreign Affairs column）などを担当。本記事は、そのコラムに掲載されたものである。なお、Friedmanはピュリッツァー賞（Pulitzer Prize）をこれまでに三度（1983, 1988, 2002）受賞している。代表作に『フラット化する社会』（2008　伏見威蕃訳、日本経済新聞社）などがある。Friedmanは同書において、テクノロジーの発展や社会変動により、人々がこれまでになく平等に容易に関わり、共同できるようになった現代世界を「フラット化した（flat）」世界と呼んだ。これに対しては反論もある。例えば、経済学者 Pankaj Ghemawat の TED におけるプレゼンテーション「本当は、フラット化していない世界（Actually the World Isn't Flat）」（http://www.ted.com）を参照。

l.40 Google　動詞としての使用。本来は名詞だが、動詞としての用法が派生している。このような品詞拡張は言語学では品詞転換（conversion）と呼ばれる。身近に探してみよう。

l.42 Gallup　「ギャラップ社」The Gallup Organization のこと。コンサルティングや世論調査などを行うアメリカの企業。名称は、前身となる the American Institute of Public Opinion を創設したアメリカの統計学者 George Gallup（1901-1984）に因む。詳細は、同社公式サイト（http://www.gallup.com/home.aspx）を参照。

l.44 the one-room schoolhouse　本文中では明示されていないが、これは John Dewey（1859-1952）の実験学校のことだと思われる。Dewey は、従来の学習（教授）形態を否定し、社会に出ていくことを見据えた作業を基盤とする授業内容を考案、それを自ら創設したシカゴ大学附属小学校で実践した。開始時、生徒16名、教師2人だった。詳細は『学校と社会』（1975　松野安男訳、岩波書店）を参照。

l.53 Accountability 2.0　2000年過ぎ頃からの新世代 Web を示す用語「Web 2.0」になぞらえた表現だろう。

l.64 Finland　フィンランドは OECD の国際生徒学習到達度調査（通称PISA）で毎回好成績を収めていることから、世界中で注目を集めている。本記事にあるように教育内容によるところはもちろん多いが、それを指導する教員の養成方法にも大きな特色があり、原動力となっている。その点については、『フィンランドは教師の育て方がすごい』が詳しい（2009　福田誠治、亜紀書房）。PISAについてはUnit 13のコラムを参照。

l.71 the Olin College of Engineering　「オーリン工科大学」アメリカのエンジニア、企業家でプロ野球選手だったFranklin W. Olin（1860-1951）の基金を基に、新たなエンジニア養成教育を目指して1997年に創設された私立大学。

l.72 the M.I.T. Media Lab　「MITメディアラボ」1985年創設の研究所。学際的に様々なプロジェクトを行っている。2014年現在の所長は日本人の伊藤穣一氏。

l.72 the 'D-school'　「Dスクール」スタンフォード大学内に2004年に設置された領域横断型のデザインスクール。

Unit 12 Need a Job? Invent It

EXERCISES

1 本文に基づいて以下の問いに英語で答えなさい。

1. Who is Tony Wagner?

2. According to Wagner, why shouldn't the goal of education today be to make every child "college ready" but "innovation ready"?

3. According to Wagner, in which country can students leave high school "innovation-ready"?

2 本文に基づいて以下の問いに答えなさい。

1. どのような生徒が知的向上を続けることができるでしょうか。

2. 21世紀型の学校とはどのようなものですか。また、そこでは校長と教師はどのような役割を果たすべきですか。また、生徒の評価方法はどうあるべきですか。

3. フィンランドの学校生活、学習はどのようなものですか。

3 CDを聴いて以下の要約文の空欄に適語を入れなさい。 2-52

Education specialist Tony Wagner says there are no more high-wage, middle-skilled jobs, only high-wage, (　　　　　) jobs. He says the goal of education today should be to make every child "(　　　　　) ready." He says young people will continue to need basic knowledge, but they will need skills and motivation even more. He says young people who are (　　　　　) motivated will learn new knowledge and skills continuously and create their own opportunities as many (　　　　　) careers disappear. He says schools teach and test things most students have no interest in, and because of this, the longer they stay in school, the (　　　　　) motivated they become. He thinks all students should have digital portfolios to show they have mastered skills like (　　　　　) thinking and communication.

4 CDをもう一度聴いてシャドーイングしてみよう。 2-52

COLUMN

　本ユニットの著者トマス・L・フリードマンによれば、現在のグローバリゼーションはバージョン3.0である（『フラット化する世界』第1章）。1492年から1800年あたりまで、つまり、コロンブスの航海をきっかけに旧世界が新世界と交易を始め、国家が勢力拡大に努めた時代に最初のグローバリゼーションは起きた。その後2000年頃までがバージョン2.0。企業の国際化、多国籍化の時代である。そして21世紀。ベルリンの壁崩壊などの国際情勢の劇的な変化やインターネットの発達により、個人が容易に世界にアクセス可能になったことでさらにバージョンアップした。フリードマンの言葉を借りれば、当初Lサイズであった地球も今やS以下だ。
　特に今世紀に入ってからのグローバリゼーションの波は激しい。19世紀、マルクスとエンゲルスは『共産党宣言』の冒頭で共産主義を「妖怪」と表現したが、「国民国家、国民経済、国民文化という三位一体」を無視するグローバリゼーションは21世紀の妖怪だと政治学者の猪口孝氏（東京大学名誉教授、新潟県立大学学長）は指摘している（『「国民」意識とグローバリズム－政治文化の国際分析』、2004、NTT出版）。

Thomas L. Friedman

UNIT 13
Arts Education in Singapore Moves to Center Stage
生きる力につながる芸術教育

By KRISTIANO ANG   May 26, 2013

芸術を専攻しても潰しがきかない。そうした考えはすでに古いものとなりつつある。この価値観の変化を可能にするシンガポールの先進的で意欲的な芸術教育の取り組みを覗いてみよう。Unit 12 と読み比べても面白いだろう。

KEYWORDS
2 - 53, 54

A. 記事読解に特に重要な語句の意味を確認しよう。

1. career prospect
2. diploma
3. monetized
4. cultural education
5. enrichment lesson
6. exam-obsessed
7. specialized faculty
8. practitioner
9. marketable skill
10. well-rounded education

B. 上下の語群で意味の近いものを結び付け、記事に現れる難易度の高い語句の言い換えを確認しよう。

1. sentiments ( )   2. hub ( )   3. heartening ( )
4. alumni ( )   5. commission ( )   6. echelon ( )
7. discipline ( )   8. flair ( )   9. permeate ( )
10. sphere ( )

a. aspect	b. portal	c. talent	d. subject
e. conception	f. spread across	g. order	h. encouraging
i. graduates	j. rank		

[1] SINGAPORE — Henry Lee wanted to be an artist, but he was worried about his **career prospects**, so he decided to study chemical engineering instead.

[2] "There's the conception that art isn't profitable, and this being Singapore, I thought I should be a good son and get a job to support the family," said Mr. Lee, 32.

[3] Now, however, his sentiments have changed, and he has gone back to school to study art.

[4] Mr. Lee does so as the art market is beginning to boom in a city-state traditionally known as a buttoned-up financial center, not a hub for creativity.

[5] Governments across Asia are pouring resources into cultural centers, museums, art schools and festivals. Singapore is no exception.

[6] The Art Stage Singapore fair, started in 2011, now draws about 120 galleries; the government has spent about 10 million Singapore dollars, or about $8 million, on an art cluster; and the National Art Gallery is scheduled to open in 2015 with one of the world's largest collections of Southeast Asian art.

[7] Interest in arts education in Singapore has also grown, from both foreign and domestic institutions.

[8] Last September, the Glasgow School of Art opened its first overseas campus, in partnership with the Singapore Institute of Technology.

[9] Not all international projects have gone smoothly, however. The Glasgow school opening came a few months before the Tisch School of the Arts, part of New York University, announced last November that it would shut its Singapore campus for financial reasons, after operating since 2007.

[10] Still, local schools have been pushing ahead in recent years. The School of Art, Design and Media at Nanyang Technological University opened in 2005. It joined more established institutions like the LaSalle College of the Arts, which opened in 1984, and the Nanyang Academy of Fine Arts, founded in 1938, where Mr. Lee is now a third-year student in its **diploma** of fine art program.

[11] NAFA has long had difficulty in drawing students to its fine art courses. The school accepts more than 700 students a year to study in areas like music and fashion design, but only 60 of them are in the fine art diploma program.

[12] "Realistically, a diploma in fine art is not something that is easily **monetized** upon graduation," said Samuel Lee, the school's academic dean. But he noted that "times have changed and it's quite heartening to see that we have now

support from parents and students."

13 **Cultural education** is also starting earlier. The state-funded School Of The Arts opened in 2008 as one of the few arts high schools in Asia. It started with 80 students a year and now admits 200.

14 "If you go to online forums, you'll see parents asking if they need to send their kids to arts **enrichment lessons** to get in," said Lim Geok Cheng, the principal.

15 Students at the School of the Arts are spared the local examination system and take the International Baccalaureate instead. "We don't have to be so **exam-obsessed**, so it's a more fertile environment for the arts," Ms. Lim said.

16 There is also a greater concentration of **specialized faculty**.

17 "The idea of the **practitioner** is central to our philosophy," said Kelly Tang, the dean for arts and a recipient of the Cultural Medallion, Singapore's highest arts prize. "We have people who are very prominent artists teaching, so students interact with living artists all the time and see the process of creating art."

18 Schools are also putting a greater effort into producing graduates with **marketable skills**. At Nanyang Academy, an illustrator might also learn digital animation, while students are encouraged to take on internships that provide work experience. The school also teaches accounting, event management and how to write business proposals.

19 "When I came to NAFA, I thought teaching was the only path afterwards," said Crystal Fong, a 21-year-old student. "But after two years, I realized you could do a lot of other things."

20 To promote its students, Nanyang Academy works with a company that connects alumni with corporations that want to commission artwork. The school also sells students' sculptures and paintings in the campus store.

21 Nanyang Academy and LaSalle have produced artists like Ming Wong and Vincent Leow who have shown work in major overseas shows like the Venice Biennale. But for now, few local art school graduates have reached the leadership echelons of Singapore's cultural institutions.

22 Art Stage Singapore is headed by Lorenzo Rudolf, the Swiss native who founded it. Eugene Tan, who started work this month as the new director of the planned National Art Gallery, is Singaporean, but was educated in Britain.

23 Singaporeans are also beginning to realize that art courses can benefit even those students who might not end up in a creative field.

24 "Singapore's education system is very exam-based," said Henry Lee, the chemical engineer-turned-art student. "But when we do art history and theory at NAFA, we are challenged to understand what is going on rather just on just memorizing events. They want us to process the facts and make it our own."

25 "Our art teachers sit alongside and have regular discussions about the curriculum with teachers from other <u>disciplines</u>," said Mr. Tang, the School of the Arts dean. "So when students look at the concept of space in art, there's a link to the concept of density or height in physics. Through things like proportion ratios and how that works in music and dance, students are able to use art as a portal to learn."

26 Mr. Tang said that the School of the Arts would be content so long as its students graduated with a **well-rounded education**.

27 "We're more than just about filling symphony seats or galleries," he said. "It's about sending people that have <u>flair</u> and a sense of imagination to other aspects of society. To be relevant, an art school has to go beyond the concert hall and <u>permeate</u> a much larger <u>sphere</u>." (976 words)

NOTES

l.18 Glasgow School of Art 1845年創立のスコットランドの芸術専門学校。

l.26 LaSalle College of the Arts 1984年創立のシンガポールの私立芸術大学。

ll.36-37 School of the Arts シンガポール初の国立中高一貫芸術専門学校。

l.43 the International Baccalaureate 「国際バカロレア」1968年創立の非営利教育財団。ジュネーブに本部がある。3歳から19歳までの生徒を対象に4つの教育プログラムを持ち、世界147カ国3,718の認定校で100万人以上の生徒がそのカリキュラムで学んでいる。フランスのバカロレアとは別。

ll.62-63 the Venice Biennale 「ヴェネチア・ビエンナーレ」1895年に始まったイタリアの国際美術展。biennnale「二年に一回（cf. biannual）」という言葉が表すように隔年開催。当初は美術展のみであったが、1930年代に、音楽（1930年）、映画（1932年）、舞台芸術（1934年）、1980年に建築、1999年に舞踊の展覧会が始まった。黒澤明監督や北野武監督の金獅子賞受賞などでもよく知られるヴェネチア国際映画祭は、ヴェネチア・ビエンナーレの映画部門として始まったものである（ライオンは、ヴェネチアの守護聖人で福音書記者の一人である聖マルコの象徴）。100年以上の歴史を持つヴェネチア・ビエンナーレは、第二次世界大戦の影響など幾多の困難を経て今に至る。その歴史については、公式サイト（http://www.labiennale.org）に詳しい情報がある。なお、「エンナーレ（ennale）」は、ラテン語の annus「一年」に由来し、annus は、annual, anniversary, anno Domini（A.D.）などの英単語と関係する。

EXERCISES

1 本文に基づいて以下の問いに英語で答えなさい。

1. Why did Henry Lee decide to study chemical engineering instead of art when he was young?

2. Why has Henry Lee gone back to school to study art?

3. According to Samuel Lee, why has the Nanyang Academy of Fine Arts long had difficulty in drawing students to its fine art courses?

2 本文に基づいて以下の問いに答えなさい。

1. 社会で通用する学生を育成するために、NAFAはどのような努力をしていますか。

2. NAFAは芸術をどのように学ばせようとしていますか。

3. NAFAで学ぶCrystal Fongは、入学の前後で将来に関してどのように考えが変わりましたか。

3 CDを聴いて以下の要約文の空欄に適語を入れなさい。 2-62

The art market in Singapore is beginning to boom, with the government (　　　　　) money into new arts centers and galleries. Interest in arts education has also grown. Schools are trying to produce graduates with (　　　　　) skills: an illustrator might also learn digital animation, while students are encouraged to do (　　　　　) that provide work experience. The school also teaches accounting, event management and how to write business proposals. One school tries to connect (　　　　　) with corporations that want to (　　　　　) artwork. It also sells students' sculptures and paintings in the campus store. There is also growing awareness that art courses can benefit students who might not end up in a creative field. Singapore's education system is very (　　　　　), but art history can help students to understand what is going on rather than just memorizing events.

4 CDをもう一度聴いてシャドーイングしてみよう。 2-62

COLUMN

シンガポールはPISAで好成績を収めていることでも知られる。これは、経済協力開発機構（Organisation for Economic Co-operation and Development：OECD）が2000年から3年おきに実施している読解、数学、科学の国際学力調査で、義務教育終了段階の15歳児を対象としている。正式名称は国際学習到達度調査（Programme for International Student Assessment）。頭文字を取ってPISAと呼ばれる。OECDの説明によれば、試験問題は学校のカリキュラムとは直接は関係なく、「義務教育終了段階の生徒がどの程度知識を実生活の中で活用でき、十分な社会参画の準備ができているかを測る」ものである。参加範囲は回を重ねるごとに広がり、直近の2012年の調査では65の国と経済圏（economy）の約51万人が調査対象となった。

2012年PISAにおけるシンガポールの生徒の平均点は、読解3位、数学2位、科学3位だった（各領域の1位はいずれも上海で、2009年から連続）。この年は、シンガポールと上海をはじめ、各領域の上位を香港、日本、韓国、台湾など東アジアが占め、国内外のメディアで大きく取り上げられた。

OECDは、調査時に生徒と学校長に学習環境などのアンケートも実施し、それを踏まえた学力調査結果の詳細な分析を行っている。分析結果とサンプル問題はOECDと国立教育政策研究所の公式サイトで公開されている。

UNIT 14

Myanmar's Educators Reach Out to the World

世界が関心を寄せるミャンマーの教育改革

By LARA FARRAR   May 5, 2013

2011年に23年に渡る軍事政権が終わり、国内の正常化に努めるミャンマー。中でも教育は最重要課題の一つだ。その復興を多くの国が支援している。その意外な意図や、支援に当たって直面している課題を読み取ろう。

KEYWORDS

2 - 63, 64

A. 記事読解に特に重要な語句の意味を確認しよう。

1. reach out   2. higher education

3. a piece of the pie   4. sexy

5. agenda   6. outreach

7. immediate needs   8. exchange

9. obstacle   10. improvement

B. 上下の語群で意味の近いものを結び付け、記事に現れる難易度の高い語句の言い換えを確認しよう。

1. refurbish ( )   2. forge ( )   3. rector ( )
4. cooperation ( ) 5. embark on ( ) 6. quadruple ( )
7. delegation ( )   8. budget ( )   9. engagement ( )
10. approval ( )

a. ties	b. resources	c. permission	d. commitment
e. start	f. representative	g. four times	h. build
i. president	j. renovate		

[1] YANGON, MYANMAR — Yangon Technological University has come a long way since it was the site of anti-government student protests in 1988 that eventually spread across Myanmar. The campus has been <u>refurbished</u> and a sense of normality is beginning to return. Undergraduate students, barred for about a decade, are back, although they all must leave by 5 p.m.; they cannot live on campus.

[2] One important question is how the university is going to <u>forge</u> links with the outside world. Like many other universities in Myanmar, Yangon Technological lacks adequate teaching materials, research facilities and updated technology, all of which a foreign partner could bring. Nyi Hla Nge, a retired <u>rector</u> at the university, said he had written a letter to the president of the Massachusetts Institute of Technology seeking to "establish <u>cooperation</u>."

[3] As Myanmar's government <u>embarks on</u> improving its **higher education** system, the possibility of assistance from foreign universities and scholars, whether in training faculty or rebuilding libraries has become a central focus. And foreign universities are pouring into the country to try to find ways to help.

[4] "Many, many major international universities would like to have **a piece of the pie**," said Jacques Fremont, director of the international higher-education program at the Open Society Foundations, a nonprofit organization founded by the investor-philanthropist George Soros.

[5] It is providing grants for scholars to teach at the University of Yangon and the University of Mandalay and to help Myanmar build an electronic library database. "It is **sexy** now to say you have a partnership with a Burmese university," Mr. Fremont said. "But the issue is: Will the Burmese say yes to everyone and then lose control of the reform **agenda**? Or will they be in a position to plan and say, 'Here is what we need?' The pressure is huge right now."

[6] Foreign institutions say the Education Ministry is showing new openness. "Our ability to engage with them has <u>quadrupled</u> over the last few months," said Andrew Leahy, a public diplomacy officer with the U.S. Embassy in Yangon who is working on exchange programs. In January, the U.S. Embassy placed the first Fulbright scholar in nearly three decades at Yangon University.

[7] In February, the European Union organized a higher-education conference with ministers, university administrators and foreign academics. The conference

was "significant" because such "open and frank discussions" had not happened before, said an E.U. representative, who requested anonymity because he did not have permission to speak to the news media.

8 EducationUSA, the U.S. State Department's **outreach** program for foreign students, held its first college fair in Myanmar in February. More than a thousand students and parents attended, as did representatives of almost a dozen U.S. universities and community colleges.

9 Also in February, a <u>delegation</u> of 10 American universities, organized by the International Institute of Education, a nonprofit group based in New York, visited Myanmar to explore partnerships. In April, the institute released a report citing some of the problems in Myanmar's education system. They included inferior physical infrastructure and technology, a lack of international ties and a political and economic system that is unable to fulfill **immediate needs**. "I think they feel a little overwhelmed," said Carola Weil, who is dean of the School of Professional and Extended Studies at American University in Washington and was part of the delegation.

10 And so do the foreign universities looking to build partnerships.

11 While some commitments were made by the delegation, including financing faculty **exchanges** and helping Myanmar universities renovate libraries, many participants said there was so much need that they did not know where to start. "The situation is much more challenging than we expected," said Denis F. Simon, vice provost for international strategic initiatives at Arizona State University. "We definitely want to do something here, but how big and how large will depend on the availability of funding."

12 Finding financing is a main **obstacle** even though Myanmar's education spending has almost tripled from $340 million in 2011 to $1 billion in the current <u>budget</u>. So far, seeking money from outside donors has not yielded much.

13 Johns Hopkins University, in Baltimore, is planning to open a center for teacher training and graduate education at the University of Yangon, but concrete plans have been put on hold until resources can be secured. "There is a commitment and a willingness to do this, but these things cost money," said Pamela Cranston, vice provost for international programs at Johns Hopkins. "People are still reluctant to get into Myanmar yet in a big way."

14 The U.S. Agency for International Development began taking applications

last November to finance higher-education projects in Myanmar. More than 200
70 organizations and individuals participated in an information session on agency grants in Washington in December. The European Union will also provide financing for faculty and student exchanges.

15 Yet foreign <u>engagement</u> still requires government <u>approval</u>. "The government said how hungry they are to have scholars from the U.S. come and visit," said
75 Christopher McCord, who is the dean of the College of Liberal Arts and Sciences at Northern Illinois University and also in the delegation. "We said, 'You have to find a way if you want us to be able to send scholars where universities don't have to go all the way to the top to get permission.'"

16 Improvements have come, even though in fits and starts, and in varied
80 ways. The campus of Yangon University was spruced up a few days before a visit by President Barack Obama last November. More important, scholars from the United States are now allowed to lecture at Yangon University for the first time in decades. (926 words)

NOTES

タイトル　Myanmar　ビルマ語の名称としては1948年の独立以来「ミャンマー」で、英語名称は「バーマ（Burma）」が軍事政権以前は公式に用いられていたが、軍事政権は、1989年に英語名もビルマ語名に合わせて「ミャンマー」に変更した。以後、国際社会では、「ミャンマー」を用いることが多い。しかし、民政回復後は、「ミャンマー」という名前の非民主的な使用の経緯から、「バーマ」が用いられることも多い。この国の国名の歴史を始め、王朝時代から現代までの歴史については、『物語ビルマの歴史』（2014　根本敬、中央公論新社）が詳しい。また、何故、世界、特にアメリカがこの国の民主化以後の復興支援に力を入れているのかについても同書は詳しい。「ミャンマー」という名称については本ユニットのコラムも参照。

l.1 Yangon　ミャンマー第一の都市で、2005年までの首都。かつてはラングーン（Rangoon）と呼ばれたが、Burma が Myanmar に変更されたのと同様に、軍政時の1989年に変更された。現在の首都はネーピードー（Naypyidaw）。

l.1 Yangon Technological University　「ヤンゴン工科大学」1924年創立のミャンマーの国立工業大学。

l.20 the Open Society Foundations　「オープン・ソサエティ財団」慈善家で投資家のGeorge Sorosにより1979年に設立された非営利組織。公式サイト（http://www.opensocietyfoundations.org/）には次のような説明がある。"The Open Society Foundations began in 1979 when George Soros decided he had enough money. His great success as a hedge fund manager allowed him to pursue his ambition of establishing open societies in place of authoritarian forms of government."

l.22 University of Yangon　「ヤンゴン大学」1920年創立のミャンマーの国立総合大学。

l.23 University of Mandalay　「マンダレー大学」1925年創立の総合大学。マンダレーはミャンマー第二の都市で、ヤンゴン以前の都。

l.24 Burmese　国名からその国の住民や言語の名を表す名詞や形容詞を作る接尾辞-eseは地理的な分布に特徴がある。該当する国名をできる限り挙げて考えてみよう。

l.32 Fulbright scholar　フルブライト交換留学制度（Fulbright Exchange Program）は、アメリカと他国の相互理解促進を目的とする制度。米上院議員J. William Fulbright（1905-1995）が提案し、1946年に制定されたフルブライト法（Fulbright Act）に基づき創設。アメリカ国務省の公式サイト（http://eca.state.gov/fulbright）によれば、現在、155カ国以上でこの制度に基づく人事交流がある。

Unit 14　Myanmar's Educators Reach Out to the World

EXERCISES

1　本文に基づいて以下の問いに英語で答えなさい。

1. What happened at Yangon Technological University in 1988?

2. What did the U.S. Embassy do in January 2013?

3. What did EducationUSA do in February 2013?

2　本文に基づいて以下の問いに答えなさい。

1. なぜ現在海外の大学はミャンマーに目を向けているのですか。

2. アメリカの10の大学の訪問団の報告書によれば、ミャンマーの大学には何が不足していますか。

3. 他国 (の大学) がミャンマーの大学を支援するにあたって、どのような問題点がありますか。

3 CDを聴いて以下の要約文の空欄に適語を入れなさい。　　　2-72

As Myanmar's government embarks on improving its (　　　　　　) education system, assistance from foreign universities has become a central focus. Foreign universities are (　　　　　　) into the country to help. Foreign institutions say the Education Ministry is showing new openness. The European Union organized a higher-education conference with ministers, university administrators and foreign academics, and the U.S. State Department's (　　　　　　) program for foreign students held its first college fair in Myanmar. But there are problems in Myanmar's education system including (　　　　　　) physical infrastructure and technology and a lack of international (　　　　　　). Johns Hopkins University, in Baltimore, wants to open a center for teacher training and graduate education but plans are on hold until it can secure (　　　　　　). U.S. scholars are now allowed to lecture at Yangon University for the first time in many years.

4 CDをもう一度聴いてシャドーイングしてみよう。　　　2-72

COLUMN

　1989年、軍事政府は国民の同意も得ず、国名の英語呼称をBurmaからMyanmarに急遽変更した。Myanmarは主要民族であるビルマ民族だけでなく他の少数民族も含めた国民全体を指すのでBurmaよりふさわしい、と軍事政府は当時その理由を説明した。だが、ビルマ近現代史の専門家である根本敬氏（上智大学外国語学部教授）によれば、どちらも狭義のビルマ民族や彼らが住む場所を本来指す言葉であり、その言い分は通らない（『物語　ビルマの歴史』序章）。

　とはいえ、政府による公式変更であったため、国連や多くのメディア、また日本を含めた多くの国が現在Myanmarと呼んでいる。その一方で、非民主的な変更の経緯から、Burmaを使い続ける立場もある。ビルマ独立運動の指導者アウンサンを父に持ち、現在の同国民主化運動指導者であるアウンサンスーチー（Aung San Suu Kyi）氏もその一人だ。2012年、軟禁から解放後初の外遊先タイとその後歴訪したヨーロッパ5カ国で自国の名をBurmaと呼び続けた際には、政府からMyanmarと呼ぶよう要請された。しかし、その後も姿勢を変えてはいない。なお、このヨーロッパ訪問中に、アウンサンスーチー氏は1991年に受賞したノーベル平和賞の受賞講演も行った。軟禁のため授賞セレモニーに出席できなかったからである。

Keywords List I

以下は、各ユニットの全キーワード一覧である。A、Bは問題の種類を示す。

Unit 1
A
- ☐ 1. manage
- ☐ 2. scrutiny
- ☐ 3. billing
- ☐ 4. swan song
- ☐ 5. sideline
- ☐ 6. cleanup
- ☐ 7. understatement
- ☐ 8. homage
- ☐ 9. acclimate
- ☐ 10. blend in

B
- ☐ 1. hallowed
- ☐ 2. equivalent
- ☐ 3. anointed
- ☐ 4. nod
- ☐ 5. fuss
- ☐ 6. bang
- ☐ 7. welling up
- ☐ 8. committed
- ☐ 9. groomed
- ☐ 10. irk

Unit 2
A
- ☐ 1. habitation
- ☐ 2. carbon monoxide
- ☐ 3. asthma
- ☐ 4. mercury poisoning
- ☐ 5. proactive
- ☐ 6. electoral system
- ☐ 7. pander
- ☐ 8. U.S.-Japan Security Treaty
- ☐ 9. acknowledge
- ☐ 10. carcinogen

B
- ☐ 1. wreathed
- ☐ 2. lift
- ☐ 3. annual
- ☐ 4. excruciating
- ☐ 5. spotless
- ☐ 6. leeway
- ☐ 7. blizzard
- ☐ 8. obstacle
- ☐ 9. toxic
- ☐ 10. incineration

Unit 3
A
- ☐ 1. plight
- ☐ 2. depopulating
- ☐ 3. parliamentary election
- ☐ 4. beneficiaries
- ☐ 5. baby diapers
- ☐ 6. hinterland
- ☐ 7. largess
- ☐ 8. malaise
- ☐ 9. affordable
- ☐ 10. conservative politicians

B
- ☐ 1. abandon
- ☐ 2. reside
- ☐ 3. stagnation
- ☐ 4. challenges
- ☐ 5. lavish
- ☐ 6. prolonged
- ☐ 7. subsidize
- ☐ 8. dismantle
- ☐ 9. incentives
- ☐ 10. shrink

Unit 4
A
- ☐ 1. rigorous
- ☐ 2. merchandise
- ☐ 3. spinach
- ☐ 4. regulate
- ☐ 5. contaminated
- ☐ 6. draconian
- ☐ 7. antibiotics
- ☐ 8. incentive
- ☐ 9. unscrupulous
- ☐ 10. conscientious

B
- ☐ 1. concerned
- ☐ 2. ship
- ☐ 3. issue
- ☐ 4. consumers
- ☐ 5. publicized
- ☐ 6. hazardous
- ☐ 7. uproar
- ☐ 8. stringent
- ☐ 9. banned
- ☐ 10. enforce

Unit 5

A
- [ ] 1. emissions
- [ ] 2. Greenhouse Effect
- [ ] 3. geologic time scale
- [ ] 4. intriguing
- [ ] 5. vindication
- [ ] 6. nail
- [ ] 7. hold up
- [ ] 8. catastrophic
- [ ] 9. augur
- [ ] 10. threshold

B
- [ ] 1. consequences
- [ ] 2. topography
- [ ] 3. degrade
- [ ] 4. instability
- [ ] 5. colleague
- [ ] 6. stabilize
- [ ] 7. compelling
- [ ] 8. disclose
- [ ] 9. implication
- [ ] 10. crucial

Unit 6

A
- [ ] 1. luck out
- [ ] 2. lull
- [ ] 3. in fits and starts
- [ ] 4. investment
- [ ] 5. futility
- [ ] 6. cherry-pick
- [ ] 7. statisticians
- [ ] 8. suspect (n.)
- [ ] 9. proffer
- [ ] 10. halcyon days

B
- [ ] 1. accumulate
- [ ] 2. variability
- [ ] 3. dismissive
- [ ] 4. make much of
- [ ] 5. staggering
- [ ] 6. trap
- [ ] 7. pollution
- [ ] 8. circulation
- [ ] 9. ultimately
- [ ] 10. prologue

Unit 7

A
- [ ] 1. e-empire
- [ ] 2. network externality
- [ ] 3. antitrust enforcement
- [ ] 4. operating system
- [ ] 5. premium price
- [ ] 6. market share
- [ ] 7. rise and fall of dynasties
- [ ] 8. barbarian
- [ ] 9. monopoly rent
- [ ] 10. creative destruction

B
- [ ] 1. geek
- [ ] 2. guru
- [ ] 3. upheaval
- [ ] 4. legend
- [ ] 5. futile
- [ ] 6. dominate
- [ ] 7. complacent
- [ ] 8. case
- [ ] 9. extract
- [ ] 10. inhibit

Unit 8

A
- [ ] 1. renewable energy
- [ ] 2. the Gulf
- [ ] 3. energy-intensive process
- [ ] 4. seawater desalination
- [ ] 5. filtration technology
- [ ] 6. cost reduction
- [ ] 7. water scarcity
- [ ] 8. the United Arab Emirates
- [ ] 9. sustainable
- [ ] 10. cost-competitive

B
- [ ] 1. steep
- [ ] 2. up-front
- [ ] 3. generate
- [ ] 4. potable
- [ ] 5. avenue
- [ ] 6. address (v.)
- [ ] 7. arm
- [ ] 8. initiative
- [ ] 9. depleting
- [ ] 10. inexorable

Unit 9

A
- [ ] 1. multinational company
- [ ] 2. European Union
- [ ] 3. recruitment
- [ ] 4. labor pool
- [ ] 5. immigration
- [ ] 6. ex-Communist country
- [ ] 7. European Commission
- [ ] 8. single market
- [ ] 9. Pan-European
- [ ] 10. hiring

B
- [ ] 1. lapse
- [ ] 2. revenue
- [ ] 3. contentious
- [ ] 4. influx
- [ ] 5. menial
- [ ] 6. meddlesome
- [ ] 7. abide by
- [ ] 8. outweigh
- [ ] 9. vexation
- [ ] 10. zilch

Unit 10

A
- [ ] 1. host the 2020 Summer Games
- [ ] 2. government debt
- [ ] 3. the rejuvenation of Japan
- [ ] 4. contamination
- [ ] 5. the Fukushima nuclear disaster
- [ ] 6. deficit spending
- [ ] 7. compact Olympics
- [ ] 8. economic recovery
- [ ] 9. Fukushima refugee
- [ ] 10. play down

B
- [ ] 1. erupt
- [ ] 2. scrutiny
- [ ] 3. containment
- [ ] 4. stricken
- [ ] 5. revelation
- [ ] 6. pall
- [ ] 7. haunting
- [ ] 8. allay
- [ ] 9. opportune
- [ ] 10. bolster

Unit 11

A
- [ ] 1. unemployment
- [ ] 2. recession
- [ ] 3. environmental concern
- [ ] 4. Olympic venue
- [ ] 5. debt
- [ ] 6. budget overrun
- [ ] 7. doping
- [ ] 8. Olympic bid
- [ ] 9. ecological consideration
- [ ] 10. deforestation

B
- [ ] 1. scramble
- [ ] 2. underused
- [ ] 3. halt
- [ ] 4. ballot
- [ ] 5. comply with
- [ ] 6. disenchantment
- [ ] 7. raze
- [ ] 8. devoid of
- [ ] 9. legacy
- [ ] 10. assessment

Unit 12

A
- [ ] 1. K-12
- [ ] 2. high-skilled job
- [ ] 3. innovation ready
- [ ] 4. critical thinking
- [ ] 5. collaboration
- [ ] 6. reimagine
- [ ] 7. education reform
- [ ] 8. intrinsic motivation
- [ ] 9. entrepreneurship
- [ ] 10. innovative economy

B
- [ ] 1. matter (v.)
- [ ] 2. sustain
- [ ] 3. obsolete
- [ ] 4. tall
- [ ] 5. elaborate (v.)
- [ ] 6. persistent
- [ ] 7. disposition
- [ ] 8. ingredients
- [ ] 9. affiliate
- [ ] 10. consortium

Unit 13

A
- ☐ 1. career prospect
- ☐ 2. diploma
- ☐ 3. monetized
- ☐ 4. cultural education
- ☐ 5. enrichment lesson
- ☐ 6. exam-obsessed
- ☐ 7. specialized faculty
- ☐ 8. practitioner
- ☐ 9. marketable skill
- ☐ 10. well-rounded education

B
- ☐ 1. sentiments
- ☐ 2. hub
- ☐ 3. heartening
- ☐ 4. alumni
- ☐ 5. commission
- ☐ 6. echelon
- ☐ 7. discipline
- ☐ 8. flair
- ☐ 9. permeate
- ☐ 10. sphere

Unit 14

A
- ☐ 1. reach out
- ☐ 2. higher education
- ☐ 3. a piece of the pie
- ☐ 4. sexy
- ☐ 5. agenda
- ☐ 6. outreach
- ☐ 7. immediate needs
- ☐ 8. exchange
- ☐ 9. obstacle
- ☐ 10. improvement

B
- ☐ 1. refurbish
- ☐ 2. forge
- ☐ 3. rector
- ☐ 4. cooperation
- ☐ 5. embark on
- ☐ 6. quadruple
- ☐ 7. delegation
- ☐ 8. budget
- ☐ 9. engagement
- ☐ 10. approval

Keywords List II

以下は各ユニットのキーワードの内、他の記事でも出現するものの一覧である。他の記事の出現箇所についてはユニット番号（U）とパラグラフ番号（P）を示し、他の記事でもキーワード（またはその一部）となっている場合には下線を施してある。なお、同一語句が現れる場合だけでなく、派生語や品詞・共起語が異なる用例も重要だと思われるものはリストに含めた。その場合にはアスタリスク（*）が付いている。複数の出現箇所を比べることで共起語句の共通性やその語句の持つ含意が感じられ、より効果的に語彙の増強ができるだろう。

Unit 1
- ☐ A1 manage
  U2P3
  U7P1* (management)
  U13P18* (management)
- ☐ A2 scrutiny
  U5P7
  U10P5
- ☐ A6 cleanup
  U2P3* (clean up, v.)
  U10P5
  U10P16
- ☐ B2 equivalent (n.)
  U6P7* (adj.)
- ☐ B8 committed
  U14P11* (commitment)
  U14P13* (commitment)

Unit 2
- ☐ A2 carbon monoxide
  U6P7* (carbon dioxide)
- ☐ A9 acknowledge
  U4P13
- ☐ B3 annual
  U9P17
- ☐ B8 obstacle
  U14P12

Unit 3
- ☐ B4 challenges
  U4P14
  U9P19
  U10P8
  U11P5
  U13P24* (v.)
- ☐ B7 subsidize
  U8P11
- ☐ B9 incentives
  U4P13

- ☐ B10 shrink
  U2P7

Unit 4
- ☐ A2 merchandise
  U9P13
- ☐ A4 regulate
  U2P6* (regulation)
- ☐ A5 contaminated
  U2P8
  U10P5
  U10P8* (contamination)
- ☐ A8 incentive
  U3P10
- ☐ B1 concerned
  U6P4* (n.)
  U7P2* (n.)
  U7P14* (n.)
  U9P11* (n.)
  U10P17* (n.)
  U11P3* (n.)
- ☐ B3 issue (n./v.)
  U2P9 (n.)
  U3P2 (n.)
  U3P3 (n.)
  U5P1 (v.)
  U9P10 (n.)
  U9P21 (n.)
  U10P16 (n.)
  U11P10 (n.)
  U14P5 (n.)
- ☐ B4 consumers
  U8P2
  U10P13
- ☐ B9 banned
  U11P8* (n.)
- ☐ B10 enforce
  U7P2* (antitrust enforcement)

Unit 5
- ☐ A1 emissions
  U2P2
  U6P2
- ☐ B5 colleague
  U10P13

Unit 6
- ☐ A3 in fits and starts
  U14P16
- ☐ A4 investment
  U2P3* (invest)
  U8P3
  U8P5
  U10P11 (investment bank)
  U10P12
  U14P4* (investor)
- ☐ A5 futility
  U7P2* (futile)
- ☐ B7 pollution
  U2P2
  U2P2* (pollution-related)
  U2P3* (pollute)
  U2P3* (pollution-control)
  U2P5
  U2P6
  U2P9
  U2P9* (pollute)
  U2P10* (pollute)

Unit 7
- ☐ A3 antitrust enforcement
  U4P12* (enforce)
- ☐ B5 futile
  U6P5* (futility)
- ☐ B6 dominate
  U6P2

Unit 8
- ☐ A9 sustainable
  U11P15* (sustainability)
  U12P2* (sustain)
- ☐ B6 address (v.)
  U3P2
  U3P8
  U3P12
- ☐ B8 initiative
  U12P11
  U14P11

Unit 9
- ☐ A2 European Union
  U14P7
  U14P14
- ☐ A4 labor pool
  U3P9* (labor market)
  U3P10* (labor force)
- ☐ A5 immigration
  U3P11
- ☐ A10 hiring
  U12P3* (hire, n.)
- ☐ B2 revenue
  U8P11 (export revenue)

Unit 10
- ☐ A1 host the 2020 Summer Games
  U11P1* (host, n.)
- ☐ A4 contamination
  U2P8* (contaminate)
  U4P4* (contaminate)
- ☐ A6 deficit spending
  U3P3* (public works spending)
  U10P13* (consumer spending)
  U14P12* (education spending)
- ☐ A8 economic recovery
  U2P1* (economic growth)
  U3P2* (economic stagnation)
  U3P6* (economic malaise)
  U3P6* (economic uncertainty)
  U8P4* (economic growth)
  U8P9* (economic growth)
  U14P9* (economic system)
- ☐ B2 scrutiny
  U1P3
  U5P7

Unit 11
- ☐ A1 unemployment
  U9P7 (unemployment rate)
- ☐ A3 environment concern
  U2P8* (environmental problems)
- ☐ A4 Olympic venue
  U10P6* (venue)
  U10P12* (venue)
- ☐ A5 debt
  U3P4
  U10P6 (government debt)
- ☐ A6 budget overrun

U10P6* (budget, v.)
- [ ] A8 Olympic bid
  U10P5* (Tokyo's bid)
  U10P12* (Tokyo's bid)
- [ ] A9 ecological consideration
  U2P7* (ecological destruction)
- [ ] B5 comply with
  U2P6
- [ ] B10 assessment
  U12P9

Unit 12
- [ ] B1 matter (v.)
  U7P6
- [ ] B2 sustain
  U8P12* (sustainable)
  U11P15* (sustainability)
- [ ] B8 ingredients
  U4P4

Unit 13
- [ ] A1 career prospect
  U9P14* (career progression)
- [ ] A2 diploma
  U12P9 (high school diploma)
- [ ] A8 practitioner
  U6P3

Unit 14
- [ ] A9 obstacle
  U2P6
- [ ] A10 improvement
  U4P10* (improve)
  U8P6
  U10P6* (improve)
  U12P9
- [ ] B7 delegation
  U11P10
- [ ] B8 budget (n.)
  U3P4
  U10P6* (v.)
  U11P5 (budget overrun)
  U11P6
- [ ] B9 engagement
  U12P7 (student engagement)

TEXT PRODUCTION STAFF

edited by
Eiichi Tamura
編集
田村 栄一

cover design by
Ruben Frosali
表紙デザイン
ルーベン・フロサリ

text design by
Ruben Frosali
本文デザイン
ルーベン・フロサリ

CD PRODUCTION STAFF

recorded by
Chris Koprowski (AmE)
Bianca Allen (AmE)
吹き込み者
クリス・コプロスキー（アメリカ英語）
ビアンカ・アレン（アメリカ英語）

Reading The New York Times 2
ニューヨークタイムズで高める英語と国際教養

2015年1月20日　初　版　発　行
2020年8月25日　第 6 刷　発　行

著　者　　小塚 良孝
　　　　　渡辺 秀樹

発行者　　佐野 英一郎

発行所　　株式会社　成美堂
　　　　　〒101-0052　東京都千代田区神田小川町3-22
　　　　　TEL 03-3291-2261　FAX 03-3293-5490
　　　　　https://www.seibido.co.jp

印刷・製本　（株）精興社

ISBN 978-4-7919-3392-1　　　　　　　　　Printed in Japan

・落丁・乱丁本はお取り替えします。
・本書の無断複写は、著作権上の例外を除き著作権侵害となります。

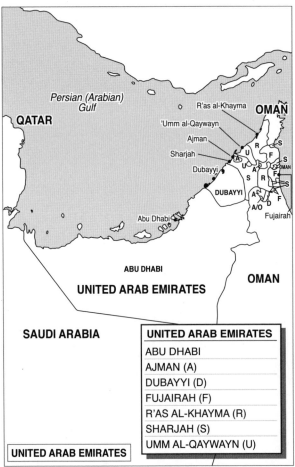
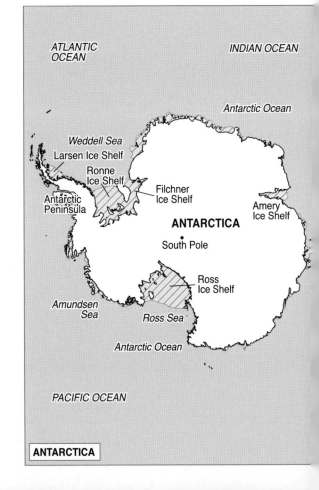